KEYS TO
VOLUNTEERING

Elizabeth Vierck

BARRON'S

This book is dedicated to Dr. Enid Opal Cox, whose life is devoted to helping others, and to the staff of the American Red Cross.

All inquiries should be addressed to:
Barron's Educational Series, Inc.
250 Wireless Boulevard
Hauppauge, NY 11788

Library of Congress Catalog Card Number 96-8758

International Standard Book Number 0-8120-9507-3

Library of Congress Cataloging-in-Publication Data
Vierck, Elizabeth, 1945– .
        Keys to volunteering / by Elizabeth Vierck.
            p.   cm. — (Barron's keys to retirement planning)
        Includes index.
        ISBN 0-8120-9507-3
        1. Voluntarism—United States. 2. Retirement—United States.
    I. Title. II. Series.
    HN90.V64V54   1996
    302′.14—dc20   96-8758
                                                    CIP

PRINTED IN THE UNITED STATES OF AMERICA

987654321

CONTENTS

ACKNOWLEDGMENTS

The author would like to thank David Appell and Karen Eiffert of the Institute of Gerontology at the University of Denver for their help on this book. In addition, Alberta Dooley, Ph.D., Assistant Professor at the University of Oklahoma School of Social Work, and Enid Opal Cox, Ph.D., Director of the Institute of Gerontology at the University of Denver, provided important insights on the design and scope of the project.

I also would like to thank the many program representatives who spent numerous hours with me on the telephone providing invaluable information about their organizations. These individuals represent the best and brightest of the wide volunteer network that serves our communities.

Last but not least, I would like to thank my untiring editor, Mary Falcon, for her good judgment, patience, and sharp editing; and Barron's director of acquisitions, Grace Freedson, for her good ideas.

PREFACE

By Dr. Enid Opal Cox
Director, Institute of Gerontology, University of Denver

Every day in communities all across the United States, volunteers provide hot meals to the homeless, help AIDS patients get to medical appointments, work to preserve historic sites, and save lives through donating their body organs. They accomplish these selfless tasks, and scores of others, through a network of organizations devoted to serving their communities. Elizabeth Vierck's *Keys to Volunteering* is a comprehensive guide to this network.

As we approach the year 2000, your work as a volunteer is increasingly important to the survival and quality of life of your fellow citizens. Cutbacks in government programs have left the challenges and responsibilities of meeting many critical needs of individuals and communities to volunteers.

Through giving to others, volunteers find that they personally benefit. A recent survey by Utah's Commission on Volunteers found that most individuals donate their time because of the good feeling that it gives them. This affirms previous research that has shown that volunteerism helps both society *and* the volunteer. Volunteering is responsible for:

- promotion of democratic processes
- the opportunity for forming meaningful associations with others in a society where relationships are often brief, shallow, and competitive

- the opportunity to learn and understand the life situations and strengths of individuals and groups of diverse culture and background
- the opportunity to work collectively with others in meaningful efforts to create a better world

Readers of this book will be pleasantly surprised to find the wide range of options available for achieving ambitions such as these in and outside of the United States. Regardless of your age, interests, physical ability, skills, or income level there is a volunteer opportunity described in the following pages that is right for you.

HOW TO USE THIS BOOK

Keys to Volunteering is designed to guide you to a successful volunteer experience. The book:
1. helps you define your interests, skills, and your volunteer options
2. provides tips on how to get the most out of your volunteer experience
3. offers a comprehensive directory of the types of volunteer projects available on national and local levels

Keys 1 and 2 in this book cover how to define your interests, motivations, and skills in order to match them with the volunteer options that are best for you. Key 3 covers how to get the most out of your volunteer experience. Key 4 explains how to guarantee that any financial contributions you make to nonprofit organizations are put to good use. Finally, Keys 5 to 41 form a comprehensive directory to the volunteer options that are available throughout the country.

Please note: In 1996 some toll free numbers will change from an 800 area code to an 888 area code. If you have trouble reaching any of the toll free numbers listed in this book, please call the toll free operator at (800) 555-1212 or (888) 555-1212 to find the new number. Also, the abbreviation TDD after a phone number means Telecommunications Device for the Deaf.

1

IDENTIFY THE RIGHT VOLUNTEER PROJECT FOR YOU

The first step to make your volunteer experience successful is to find the niche that is right for you. For example, if you are interested in environmental issues but your volunteer project involves working with local politicians who are fighting to prevent protection of endangered species, you are in the wrong spot. In contrast, if you have a burning desire to teach and to help disadvantaged children and you are volunteering to tutor "at risk" youth, you are in the right spot.

Here is a checklist of questions to use to identify the right volunteer project for you. You might want to make a copy of this list and answer the questions on a separate piece of paper.

Given a choice to do anything you wanted, what would it be? Regardless of how you answer this question, as long as it does not involve doing harm to anyone or anything, there is a volunteer option out there for you. For example, do you prefer to cook more than anything else? Every hospital, nursing home, homeless shelter, or other institution in your area would welcome your culinary skills. Do you prefer to be in the great outdoors? The American Hiking Society, which works to preserve America's wilderness trails, might be your answer. Did you promise yourself that once you retired you would take up scuba diving and foreign travel? Then Oceanic Society Expeditions, where you can scuba dive in Hawaii and track dolphins, may be your answer.

1

How much time do you have to offer now?
Even if you have only two hours a month to donate to volunteering, there is an organization in your area that would welcome that contribution of time. For example, in two hours you could serve a hot meal in a soup kitchen, stuff 500 envelopes for your local United Way drive, transport one or more disabled persons to the polls to vote, or visit some elderly people in a nursing home.

How much time will you have to offer in the future?
If you do not have a lot of time to offer now, but you will have more in the future, you might want to start now by donating your efforts to several different organizations. That way when you can devote more time, you will know which organizations are best for you.

What are your reasons for volunteering?
In order to get the most out of your volunteer time, you should examine your motives and make sure you don't have unrealistic expectations. For example, some people volunteer in order to spark up their social lives and are disappointed when they don't meet enough new people in their volunteer positions. Others have a high sense of duty and carrying out a needed task makes them feel that they are contributing a great deal. Still others desire variety in their lives and are happy just to spend time on something that is outside of their normal routine.

Here are some common motivations for volunteering that you might experience. You might have a desire to:
- meet new people
- learn new skills
- pass skills on to another generation
- stop something, such as drunk driving
- prevent something, such as crime
- find a solution to a problem, such as a cure for breast cancer, AIDS, or heart disease

- carry out a sense of duty
- give something back to your community
- help people who are not as well off as you physically, financially, or in other ways
- fill time
- develop a job opportunity
- add variety to life

Pulling It Together

Once you have answered the preceding questions, the next step is to flip through Keys 5 to 41 and the index in the back of the book to find the volunteer options that match your interests and motivations.

Depending on your needs, you may find that you can stick to one Key or you may want to look through a number of them. For example, if your interest is in helping the disadvantaged, you could look over Keys 7, 9, 10, 11, 12, 18, and 19. However, if you want to help the disadvantaged specifically using your skills as a lawyer, then you could limit your reading to Key 9. In any case, before you undertake a volunteer activity or donate money to an organization, be sure to read Keys 2, 3, and 4.

2

IDENTIFY THE SKILLS
YOU HAVE TO OFFER

In Key 1 you identified your area of interest and your motivations for volunteering. It is also important to assess how you will spend your time while volunteering. Sometimes your skills and your area of interest are one and the same; often they are not.

Some words of caution: If you have skills to offer that you would prefer *not* to be doing, don't get pigeonholed in an area that you don't want to be in. For example, let's say you are a whiz at typing, but you have been a secretary for 30 years and you are sick and tired of office work. Make it clear to the volunteer coordinator that you want to do something else and that you want to be called on to do secretarial work only in a real pinch.

You may be unaware that the skills you have could help others. Here are two examples.

A couple of years ago one gentleman, Sam Knowles, mentioned to the volunteer coordinator at a community center, "I'd love to figure out how to get the kids in our neighborhood off the streets. They don't have anything to do all day but hang out on the corner and get in trouble. But I don't have anything to offer them as an alternative." The volunteer coordinator remembered that Mr. Knowles had owned an auto repair shop for over 50 years, and got him a position helping at-risk youths in a technical school. He now runs a very successful after-school program in a neighborhood garage.

Betty Wolfe, who attended the same community center, also didn't think she had anything to offer a charitable organization. But with the help of her volunteer coordinator, she started donating her time in an arts and crafts program in a homeless shelter. With her knowledge of sewing and knitting, she has become a big hit among girls age 8 to 13, who call her, with great affection, Aunt Singer, in honor of the sewing machine that she donated to the shelter.

In short, volunteering often brings out the best in the individual, and when you become devoted to a project you may find that you have skills of which you are not aware. The story of the founding of the organization Mothers Against Drunk Driving (MADD) is a classic example of this phenomenon. Thirteen-year-old Cari Lightner was walking to a church activity in May 1980 when she was struck and killed by a drunk driver. At the time her grief-stricken mother, Candy Lightner, was not even registered to vote. Political action was the farthest thing from her mind. However, Ms. Lightner put her grief into action and started Mothers Against Drunk Driving. Today, thanks to her hard work and extraordinary organizational and motivational skills, there are over 300 chapters of MADD, which have literally changed public opinion and public policies about drunk drivers.

Identify Your Skills
Here is a brief list of some skills that you could offer a volunteer organization.
- administrative skills, such as answering phones, typing, computer entry, filing, organizing, stuffing envelopes, preparing publication materials
- artistic skills, drafting, drawing, making posters and promotional materials
- athletic and outdoor skills, such as hiking and building trails or working in national parks
- computer skills, such as setting up an office computer system
- construction, carpentry, plumbing, and related skills

- cooking, meal preparing, meal serving
- driving, running errands
- friendly visiting, providing companionship
- management skills
- organizational skills
- public relations
- research, data collection, analysis
- teaching, tutoring
- writing proposals or promotional materials
- writing letters to senators, congress people, city councilors, governors, and so on

If you can't identify with any skills in this list, try this exercise: Ask three people who know you well what skills they think you have to offer a charitable organization. Their answers are your answers.

3

MAXIMIZE YOUR VOLUNTEER EXPERIENCE

In order to get the most out of your experience, it is helpful to follow some guidelines when you are first getting started with your investigation into potential volunteer activities. Following these guidelines will help ensure that there will not be any unwelcome surprises down the road.

Here are some points that you should go over with volunteer coordinators at all organizations that you are considering. They will help you determine whether you want to go forward or look for another option.

Before you sign up with a particular organization
- Meet and talk to a few members; attend a couple of meetings; and read the organization's newsletter, if they have one, to determine if it is the right place for you.
- Ask a series of questions to make sure that the organization's philosophy and structure does not conflict with your attitudes and beliefs. Here is a checklist:
  1. Find out what the organization's goal is.
  2. Find out if anyone is restricted from joining the organization for any reason, such as race, ethnic origin, occupation, or religious beliefs.
  3. Find out who runs the organization. Do you have a good feeling about them? Ask around about their reputation.
  4. Find out where the money comes from to run the organization. For example, if funding comes from the tobacco industry and the organization conducts research on the causes of cancer, you might be suspicious of their goals.

5. Find out if anyone representing the organization has been arrested for any reason. Find out if violence has ever been used to make a point or to serve the interest of the organization. If so, turn away from that place.
6. Look at the organization's budget. It will reveal what its priorities are.
7. Check with your local volunteer center, such as your city or state's United Way office, to find out what type of reputation the organization has and how it treats volunteers.

When you start making arrangements to take on a specific volunteer project, ask these questions:
- What will my responsibilities be?
- Will I be trained to do my volunteer job?
- Who will I report to?
- Will I have to turn in reports or records?
- What equipment, if any, will I have to use?
- Who else will be working with me?
- Have there been any problems in this area that I should know about?
- Will someone let me know how I'm doing, in case I need to make changes in how I do my job?

Do You Need a Contract?

Many volunteers and organizations that rely on volunteers prefer to sign volunteer contracts. Volunteer coordinators often believe that such contracts provide a greater opportunity for success for both the volunteer and the organization, because they eliminate problems later. Such contracts can include:
- name and address of the volunteer and the volunteer organization
- job title
- job description

- length of time of the contract
- an agreement to cover the volunteer for liability insurance and workman's compensation in case of an accident
- materials and assistance that the organization agrees to provide to make the volunteer's job worthwhile (displays for fairs, necessary administrative help, and so on)
- training that will be provided, if any
- expenses that will be covered, if any

If at First You Don't Succeed

Not all volunteer jobs are successful right away. You may donate your time to several organizations before you find the one that is right for you, or you may have to try several different positions within the same organization before you find the niche where you are most comfortable. Don't give up. There are many good organizations in need of your help, but it may take time to find the right one for you.

One option to consider is starting your own organization, or starting a chapter of an existing organization in your area. Many national organizations provide training and assistance with starting new chapters or groups.

One way to get started is to talk to your closest volunteer office and find out where the program gaps are in your city or state. For example, do you have an interest in consumer issues? If there is not a Call for Action program in your area, in which trained volunteer mediators work to resolve consumer complaints, you could contact CFA's national headquarters to find out how to get a program started in your area. Are you interested in the rights of older women, but there aren't any organized women's groups in your area? Call the Older Women's League national office.

4

MAKE WISE FINANCIAL CONTRIBUTIONS AND AVOID FRAUD

Most volunteer jobs have some expenses associated with them such as transportation costs to and from the volunteer site or annual dues. In addition, most volunteer organizations rely on the goodwill of their donors to survive. Deciding where to contribute your hard-earned dollars is often very difficult.

There are some guidelines to follow for how much money individuals typically give nonprofit organizations. The Independent Sector, an organization that studies volunteerism, suggests that everyone should give 5 percent of their incomes to the causes they believe in. Many religious organizations suggest that their members tithe (commit 10 percent of their income) annually to them. These guidelines are easier to follow for some people than for others. For example, if you are living on a fixed income they are probably unrealistic.

Before you contribute money to an organization check with the Philanthropic Advisory Service (PAS) of your local or state Better Business Bureau. They will know about organizations that are not on the up-and-up. In addition, check with the National Charities Information Bureau (NCIB), which evaluates most charities according to a carefully chosen list of standards. Contact them at:

National Charities Information Bureau
19 Union Square
New York, NY 10003
(212) 929-6300

Many fraudulent organizations have certain tricks they use to bilk well-intentioned philanthropists out of their hard-earned dollars, including using sound-alike names such as the Arthritis Fund, to sound like the Arthritis Foundation, or the National Association of Retired People, to sound like the American Association of Retired Persons.

One charity scam that was prominent recently involved phone calls in which con artists claimed to be from the Police Officer's Recovery Fund, or a similar sounding organization. They targeted older people, who as a group are known to be generous, and asked for $10 or more for scholarship funds for the children of injured policemen. The checks went to a post office box and were cashed by the con artists.

Guidelines for Donating Money
Here are some guidelines to follow to avoid becoming a victim of fraud when you receive requests to donate money at your door or by telephone:

- *Never* give cash or a credit card number to a door-to-door solicitor. If you do contribute, make out your check in the name of the organization, not the individual doing the collecting.
- When you receive a call asking for donations, don't give out your credit card number or agree to send the caller a check. Ask them to mail you materials about their solicitation. (Every reputable organization has written materials that they can send you.) If they don't agree to do this, do not send any money to any address they give you. If they do mail you materials, and you check into their reputation and you like what you find, the organization will welcome your money at that time.
- You can also tell the organization's representative to call you back in a week after you have had time to consider their request. In the meantime, check the organization

out with the BBB's Philanthropic Advisory Service and the National Charities Information Bureau (NCIB), listed earlier in this key, before you send them any money.

- If you are asked to purchase a promotional item such as a T-shirt, candy, cookies, or tickets, find out what percentage of your costs are actually tax deductible and what percentage actually goes to the charity.
- If you suspect that you have been a victim of tele-marketing fraud, contact the Alliance Against Fraud in Telemarketing, part of the National Consumer's League in Washington, DC, at (202) 835-3323.

Here are some guidelines to follow when you receive solicitations in the mail:

- Is the mailing disguised in some way as a bill? This is illegal unless the solicitation states clearly that it is an appeal that you have a right to refuse.
- Did you receive something that you didn't order and the organization wants a donation in return? This is also illegal. You are not obligated to pay for stamps with your name on them, note pads, greeting cards, or anything else that you receive in the mail that you did not request.
- Does the organization fraudulently use a name similar to another organization such as those mentioned earlier in this key? In this case, let the legitimate organization know that you have received a fraudulent solicitation. Also inform the Better Business Bureau's Philanthropic Advisory Service listed above. Save the materials you received as evidence.

Keeping Records
Remember, many of your expenses for your volunteer position are tax deductible. However, it is important to keep records to document your expenses for the IRS. Unfortunately, you cannot deduct the value of the time

you donate. Be sure to check with your accountant or a volunteer organization representative to clarify exactly which items are tax deductible. Here is a list of the records you should keep for items that *may* be tax deductible:

- transportation stubs
- receipts and canceled checks for items used directly for the volunteer project
- receipts and canceled checks for seminars and training programs
- receipts and canceled checks for direct donations
- receipts and canceled checks for membership dues

5

VOLUNTEER WITH AARP OR OTHER SENIOR GROUPS

Most organizations for older people are built on the principles of volunteerism. In other words, members of these groups work for the common good of all generations through donations of time and money. For example, the American Association of Retired Persons (AARP) is known for its volunteer action in numerous areas including development of public policy and provision of practical, hands-on programs such as tax assistance for retired people. The National Council on Aging runs a number of valuable volunteer programs, such as the Family Friends program, in which older people provide tender loving care to disabled children. And the Older Women's League is dedicated to bettering the lives of older women.

The following senior organizations provide a wealth of opportunities for volunteering on both a national and community level.

American Association of Retired Persons (AARP)

AARP encourages older people to volunteer. Its Volunteer Talent Bank matches potential volunteers to opportunities. AARP offers a wide range of volunteer activities. Examples of the issues you can volunteer for are literacy, the environment, tax assistance, legal assistance, arts and culture, legislation, health care, and housing.

AARP Fulfillment
601 E St. NW
Washington, DC 20049
(202) 434-3219

Catholic Golden Age (CGA)

CGA is devoted to the interests of senior Catholics in the United States. CGA has chapters across the United States, and, among other things, funds research on aging. To find out how you can join CGA contact:

Catholic Golden Age, National Headquarters
430 Penn Ave.
Scranton, PA 18503
(717) 342-3294
(800) 836-5699

Families USA Foundation

Families USA is a national consumer organization that works on issues important to the elderly, as well as those important to all age groups, such as affordable health care and long-term care. The foundation's grassroots lobbying organization, ASAP, works at the local level to influence legislation. For information about Families USA, contact:

Families USA Foundation
1334 G St. NW
Washington, DC 20005
(202) 628-3030

Foster Grandparent Program (FGP)

FGP matches volunteers over age 60 with needy children. Foster Grandparents help children on an individual basis for a total of 20 hours a week. The program is run by the Corporation for National and Community Services (formerly ACTION). All volunteers receive training and may receive a stipend. Contact the following to find out the regional office near you:

The Corporation for National and Community Service
1100 Vermont Ave. NW
Washington, DC 20525
(202) 606-5000

Generations United (GU)

This organization is a good resource for locating volunteer programs that focus on older and younger generations working together.

Generations United
c/o CWLA
440 First St. NW, Suite 310
Washington, DC 20001-2085
(202) 638-2952

Gray Panthers

The Gray Panthers is dedicated to bringing together different generations, and people of all ethnic, racial, and cultural backgrounds. The Panthers have organizations in communities throughout the United States. They work on such issues as affordable housing and health care on both national and local levels. To find out how you can join the Gray Panthers contact:

Gray Panthers
2025 Pennsylvania Ave. NW, Suite 821
Washington, DC 20006
(202) 466-3132
(800) 280-5362

National Council on the Aging (NCOA)

NCOA is dedicated to improving the quality of life of older people. NCOA divisions work in the areas of adult day care, senior centers, long-term care, senior housing, senior employment, and health promotion. For more information about NCOA, contact:

National Council on the Aging
409 Third St. SW
Washington, DC 20024
(202) 479-6675

National Council of Senior Citizens (NCSC)

NCSC has more than 5,000 affiliated clubs in the United States. Among other things, members lobby for legislation important to older people and work to reserve and improve programs such as Medicare and Social Security. For information about how to join NCSC, contact:

National Council of Senior Citizens
1331 F St. NW
Washington, DC 20004
(202) 347-8800

National Retiree Volunteer Coalition (NRVC)

NRVC's mission is to mobilize and train retirees to develop and run Corporate Retiree Volunteer Programs for community leadership and service. Volunteers assist corporations in addressing communities' critical needs, such as educating children, assisting the disabled, and caring for the elderly. To find out more about the coalition, contact:

National Retiree Volunteer Coalition
4915 W. 35th St.
St. Louis Park, MN 55416
(612) 920-7788

Older Women's League (OWL)

This group of middle-aged and older women includes 120 local groups that address issues important to their well-being. (For more information on OWL, see Key 36.) To find a group near you, look in your local telephone directory under Older Women's League, or contact:

Older Women's League
666 11th St. NW, Suite 700
Washington, DC 20001
(202) 783-6686

Retired and Senior Volunteer Program (RSVP)

In this program almost 500,000 older people volunteer on a range of social issues such as crime prevention, working with the homeless, and counseling youth. The program is run by the Corporation for National and Community Services (formerly ACTION). Contact the following to find out the regional office near you:

The Corporation for National and Community Service
1100 Vermont Ave. NW
Washington, DC 20525
(202) 606-5000

Senior Companion Program (SCP)

SCP volunteers help other older people in need. The majority assist people who are homebound. The program is run by the Corporation for National and Community Services (formerly ACTION). Contact the following to find out the regional office near you:

The Corporation for National and Community Service
1100 Vermont Ave. NW
Washington, DC 20525
(202) 606-5000

Seniors in Service to Seniors

This program, sponsored by the Points of Light Foundation, encourages older Americans to volunteer by identifying at-risk seniors and helping them get the services they need.

Seniors in Service to Seniors
Points of Light Foundation
1737 L St. NW
Washington, DC 20036
(202) 223-9186

6

VOLUNTEER WITH A SERVICE CLUB

Service clubs are often organized with volunteer purposes in mind. For example, the Lions Club motto is "we serve," Rotary Clubs are organized with the aim of providing humanitarian service, and Moose International's goal is to improve community life. Most service clubs welcome older and retired members, although some memberships are by invitation only. This key lists a variety of service clubs.

Federation for Woman's Exchanges (FWE)

FWE is an association of Woman's Exchanges that operate voluntary nonprofit consignment shops. Woman's Exchanges stores sell high-quality handcrafts and home-cooked foods, and the profits are given to nonprofit organizations. To find out how to start a shop in your area contact:

Federation for Woman's Exchanges
51 Woods Lane
Scarsdale, NY
(914) 725-0228

Kiwanis International (KI)

Kiwanis represents 8,700 local groups of business and professional individuals. Each club sponsors its own service projects. Among other things, the clubs seek to provide assistance to the young and elderly, develop community facilities, and foster international understanding and goodwill. Call the KI toll free number to find a program near you, or look in your local telephone directory under Kiwanis Club.

Kiwanis International
3636 Woodview Trace
Indianapolis, IN 46268
(317) 875-8755
(800) 549-2647

The Links

This organization of women is committed to the community through educational, cultural, and civic activities. Through 40 state groups, the Links supports charitable activities and a Grant-in-Aid program. Contact the Links office in Washington, DC, to find a program near you:

The Links
1200 Massachusetts Ave. NW
Washington, DC 20005
(202) 842-8686

Lions Club International (LCI)

This multinational organization of 1.4 million members represents business and professional men and women in 180 countries. There are over 40,000 clubs throughout the world. The Lions Clubs provide community service through such programs as blindness prevention, work with the deaf, and drug awareness. To find a program near you, look in your local telephone directory under Lions Club or contact:

Lions Club International
300 22nd St.
Oak Brook, IL 60521
(708) 571-5466

National Assistance League (NAL)

NAL's 80 chapters "act as a friend at any and all times to men, women, and children in need of care, guidance, and assistance." Each chapter selects at least one self-sustaining philanthropic project such as geriatric programs or help for the hearing impaired. To find a program near you, look in your local telephone directory under National Assistance League or contact:

National Assistance League
P.O. Box 5127
High Point, NC 27262
(910) 869-2166

Rotary International

Founded in 1905, the Rotary Club was the first service organization in the world. Rotary's membership is by invitation only, and includes professionals and executives. To join Rotary it is necessary to contact a present member to sponsor you. To find a program near you, look in your local telephone directory under Rotary Club or contact:

Rotary International
One Rotary International
1500 Sherman Ave.
Evanstown, IL 60201
(708) 866-3000

Sertoma International (SI)

This civic club of business and professional men and women provides services to persons with communication disorders. To find an SI program near you contact:

Sertoma International (SI)
1912 East Meyer Blvd.
Kansas City, MO 64132
(816) 333-8300
(800) 593-5646

Seroptomists International of the Americas (SIA)

This multinational organization of professional and business women has 50,000 members in about 1,500 clubs. Areas of interest include economic and social development, education, environment, health, human rights, and the status of women. Membership in a Seroptomist Club is by invitation only. To find a program near you, look in your local telephone directory under Seroptomists International of the Americas.

Seroptomists International of the Americas
1616 Walnut St., Suite 700
Philadelphia, PA 19103
(215) 732-0512

7

VOLUNTEER TO IMPROVE HOUSING

When you volunteer to improve dilapidated or inadequate housing, you are bettering the quality of life for its residents and future residents. Two excellent organizations provide a great example. The highly successful program, Christmas in April, renovates over 2,400 homes across the country every year using volunteer labor and donated materials. Second, former President Jimmy Carter and his wife Rosalynn's involvement in the volunteer program Habitat for Humanity has made it one of the best known volunteer programs in the country. Habitat for Humanity renovates housing in the United States and overseas. It now has 700 affiliates across the country.

Christmas in April

Volunteers for Christmas in April help repair the homes of low-income individuals, especially those who are elderly or disabled. The concept behind the organization's name is that one day each year, usually in April, volunteers get together and renovate homes and nonprofit facilities using donated materials. Christmas in April has 165 programs in 46 states. Call their toll free number to find a program near you or to find out how to start a program in your area

Christmas in April
1225 I St. NW, Suite 601
Washington, DC 20005
(202) 326-8268
(800) 473-4229

Habitat for Humanity International

Habitat for Humanity International was started by Millard and Linda Fuller in 1976 with the goal of building decent housing for people who do not have it. Habitat is active in more than 1,100 cities in 40 countries. The families who receive the homes help with the building, and work side by side with volunteers who do everything from fund-raising to shingling.

Habitat for Humanity International
121 Habitat St.
Americus, GA 31709-3498
(912) 924-6935
(800) HABITAT

Housing Assistance Council (HAC)

HAC's goal is to increase housing for low-income people in rural areas. HAC operates in every state.

Housing Assistance Council
1025 Vermont Ave. NW, Suite 606
Washington, DC 20005
(202) 842-8600

National Housing Institute (NHI)

NHI is an advocate for housing for moderate and low-income people. They are particularly interested in volunteers with a background in publishing and research.

National Housing Institute
439 Main St.
Orange, NJ 07050
(201) 678-3110

National Low Income Housing Coalition (NLIHC)
NLIHC works to make the public aware of the need for low-income housing for low-income people.

National Low Income Housing Coalition (NLIHC)
1012 14th St. NW, Suite 1200
Washington, DC 20005
(202) 662-1530

NeighborWorks
These programs reflect local needs and vary from community to community. The programs work with low-income people who need affordable housing. Volunteers may take part in all aspects from fund-raising to weatherizing homes. NeighborWorks is active in over 350 neighborhoods nationwide. If your community has a program it will be listed in your local telephone book under the name NeighborWorks or Neighborhood Services.

8

VOLUNTEER TO BEAUTIFY YOUR COMMUNITY

There are many things that you can do to keep an attractive community looking great or to beautify a blighted neighborhood.

- Volunteer to clean up local parks, playgrounds, streams, and beaches. Clean up graffiti, pick up garbage and litter, repair broken equipment and fences, and plant trees and gardens.

- Get a group together to adopt an area and keep it beautiful. For example, you could get together on the first Saturday morning of each month and meet at your local park for a two-hour organized cleanup, or, if you live near a lake, your group could spend a couple of hours once a month cleaning up and raking the beach and surrounding area.

- Call attention to your efforts by getting your Mayor or City Council to declare a particular day "Keep Your Community Beautiful Day." Get your local paper to publicize it. Organize a neighborhood pot luck dinner at the end of the day.

- Pick a day (or days) each year when you and your neighbors plant trees and gardens. Then get volunteers to follow up with taking care of them on a regular basis.

- Many local departments of parks and recreation sponsor tree planting programs. Check with the department in your area for advice on how to organize such a program in your area.

The following list covers resources for getting involved with some volunteer organizations in your community to beautify the landscape, plant gardens and trees, and keep rivers, streams, and beaches clean.

Beautifying the Landscape

Scenic America

This organization works to protect America's scenic heritage. Its goal is to clean up visual pollution through such measures as controlling billboards along highways, helping communities protect their appearance, and establishing a coast-to-coast scenic highway.

Scenic America
21 Dupont Circle
Washington, DC 20036
(202) 833-4300

Planting Gardens and Trees

American Forestry Association (AFA)

AFA is the oldest conservation association in the United States. AFA members work to create public lands and parks, and promote conservation. AFA's national Global Releaf program creates or improves forests through tree planting, conservation, and legislative reform.

American Forestry Association (AFA)
P.O. Box 2000
Washington, DC 20013-2000
(202) 667-3300

American Free Tree Program (AFTP)

This popular program is well on its way to its goal of establishing 1,000 projects and to plant one billion trees nationwide. AFTP's theme is "A responsible citizen is one who will plant one tree every year of his life." AFTP will show people how to start their own programs using volunteers and local funding.

American Free Tree Program
P.O. Box 9079
Canton, OH 44711
(216) 456-TREE
(800) 686-1886 (no tree orders please)

The Gardeners of America, Inc. (TGOA)

TGOA's 150 clubs across the country put on garden shows, clinics, tours, and beautification projects. "Gardening from the Heart" is a horticultural therapy program sponsored by TGOA for people in institutions such as nursing homes and for those with special needs.

The Gardeners of America, Inc. (TGOA)
5560 Merle Hay Road
Johnston, IA 50131-0241
(515) 278-0295

National Arbor Day Foundation (NADF)

NADF has three programs—the Arbor Day Celebration, Trees for America, and Tree City USA—that are carried out at the local level by volunteer groups. The Trees for America campaign provides ten trees for planting to each person who joins the Foundation. For information about this program and others, contact:

National Arbor Day Foundation
100 Arbor Ave.
Nebraska City, NE 68410
(402) 474-5655

National Council of State Garden Clubs (NCSGC)

The NCSGC includes over 8,000 clubs and more than 260,000 members in the United States and abroad. Each club has its own character and focus such as garden design, recycling, or historic preservation.

National Council of State Garden Clubs
4401 Magnolia Ave.
St. Louis, MO 63110-3492
(314) 776-7574

National Gardening Association (NGA)

NGA matches garden-based educational programs in schools, called GrowLabs, with community groups who provide funding and volunteer assistance. The association publishes the *Growing Ideas* newsletter.

National Gardening Association
180 Flynn Ave.
Burlington, VT 05401
(802) 863-1308

TreePeople

This organization is dedicated to showing citizens how to plant and maintain trees. Its Citizen Forester Training Program provides tree planting advice and technical training to communities.

TreePeople
Cold Water Canyon
12601 Mulholland Drive
Beverly Hills, CA 90210
(818) 753-4600

Rivers, Streams, and Beaches

American Rivers
This membership organization works to preserve and restore rivers and landscapes. Founded in 1973, American Rivers has helped restore thousands of miles of natural rivers.

American Rivers
1025 Vermont Ave. NW, Suite 720
Washington, DC 20005
(202) 547-6900

Center for Marine Conservation (CMC)
CMC sponsors International Coastal Cleanup Day, which is held on the third Saturday in September. On Cleanup Day volunteers clean up beaches and coastal areas along inland lakes and rivers. To learn more about this program and CMC's other volunteer projects contact:

Center for Marine Conservation
1725 DeSales St. NW, Suite 500
Washington, DC 20036
(202) 429-5609

RiverNetwork
RiverNetwork is a great resource for finding out about river conservation activities in your community. They will also help you set up a group if there is not one established near you. RiverNetwork also has a land conservancy program. For information call their toll free number:

RiverNetwork
P.O. Box 8787
Portland, OR 97207-8787
(503) 241-3506
(800) 423-6747

9

PROVIDE LEGAL AND MEDIATION ASSISTANCE

This key covers two volunteer areas—legal services and mediation assistance.

Legal Services

If you are a lawyer, paralegal, or have any legal experience, you can provide a valuable service to members of your community who can not afford legal services through volunteering at your local legal services organization or clinic (listed in your local phone book under community or legal services). For example, providing advice on how to get a restraining order against an abusive husband, explaining how to file for Social Security disability payments, or answering questions about tenant rights are all important services you could perform.

Here are some resources for volunteering in legal services:

American Civil Liberties Union (ACLU)

The ACLU is dedicated to preserving and defending the principles of individual liberty and equality embodied in the Constitution and U.S. civil rights laws. It is composed of two organizations: the ACLU Foundation, which handles legal work and conducts public education programs; and ACLU, which carries out legislative lobbying. The ACLU depends heavily on volunteers. There are hundreds of local chapters across the country. Check in your local telephone book to see if there is a chapter near you or contact:

American Civil Liberties Union
National Headquarters
132 W. 43rd St.
New York, NY 10036
(212) 944-9800

Court Appointed Special Advocate Program (CASA)

CASA volunteers are advocates for abused and neglected children who have been placed in foster care. There are more than 550 CASA programs in the United States. Volunteer advocates are needed to conduct interviews with parents and other key people, review records, and make recommendations on behalf of the children for whom they are advocates. They often appear in court. Volunteers receive training. Check in your local phone book to see if there is a CASA program near you, or call the National Court Appointed Special Advocate Association toll free number:

The National Court Appointed
  Special Advocate Association
2722 Eastlake Ave. East, Suite 220
Seattle, WA 98102
(206) 328-8588
(800) 628-3233

Lambda Legal Defense and Education Fund, Inc.

Lambda advocates the rights of lesbians and gay men and advocates education about discrimination based on sexual orientation. Volunteer attorneys work on test cases of discrimination in housing, employment, immigration, and the military; AIDS-related issues; and constitutional rights.

Lambda Legal Defense and Education Fund, Inc.
Western Regional Office
6030 Wilshire Blvd., Suite 200
Los Angeles, CA 90036-3617
(213) 937-2728

Volunteer Lawyers for the Arts (VLA)

VLA volunteers provide free legal assistance on art-related matters, such as contracts and labor relations, to artists who cannot afford legal fees. VLA has affiliates in over 40 cities across the country.

Volunteer Lawyers for the Arts
1 East 53rd St.
New York, NY 10022
(212) 319-2787

Mediation Assistance

Mediation is a form of dispute resolution in which individuals who have a conflict arrive at a mutually acceptable settlement. Mediation is often carried out by a trained volunteer who is neutral and writes up the agreement once it is carried out. If you are interested in becoming a mediator, the following organizations can help you find local resources for training. Examples of the types of cases you might work on are family disputes, trespassing, child custody, victim-offender disputes, landlord-tenant disputes, and patients vs. health institutions, such as nursing homes.

Here are some resources for volunteering for mediation programs:

American Bar Association (ABA)
Standing Committee on Dispute Resolution

The American Bar Association publishes the *American Bar Association Dispute Resolution Program Directory,* which lists local organizations that use volunteer mediators.

Standing Committee on Dispute Resolution
American Bar Association
740 15th St. NW
Washington, DC 20061
(202) 662-1000

Call for Action (CFA)

CFA sponsors a free, confidential consumer hotline run by volunteers. The program operates as a nonprofit affiliate of radio and TV broadcasters across the country. Trained volunteer mediators take consumer complaints and then work to resolve them. Contact the national headquarters to find out if there is a Call for Action program at one of your local stations.

Call for Action
3400 Idaho Ave. NW
Washington, DC 20016
(202) 537-0585 (202) 537-1551 (TDD)

Conflict Resolution Center International (CRCI)

If you would like to know about mediation programs in your area, CRCI's clearinghouse and resource center will provide you with the information you need. Contact them at:

Conflict Resolution Center International
7101 Hamilton Ave.
Pittsburgh, PA 15208-1828
(412) 371-9884

Council of Better Business Bureaus (CBBB)
Alternative Dispute Resolution (ADR) Division

CBBB's Alternative Dispute Resolution (ADR) Division provides help with disputes between customers and companies. Many local Bureaus offer the program. Currently there are over 9,000 certified volunteer arbitrators across the country. Volunteer arbitrators receive a training course. Contact your local CBBB, listed under Better Business Bureau in your local telephone directory, to see if there is a program near you or contact:

Council of Better Business Bureaus
National Headquarters
4200 Wilson Blvd.
Arlington, VA 22203
(703) 276-0100

National Institute for Dispute Resolution (NIDR)
Like CRCI, NIDR will provide you with information about mediation programs in your area.

National Institute for Dispute Resolution
1726 M St. NW
Washington, DC 20036
(202) 466-4764

PACT Institute of Justice
Victim-Offender Reconciliation Program (VORP)
VORP volunteer mediators arbitrate with crime victims and offenders to work out agreements about restitution. Volunteers receive extensive training. The Pact Institute of Justice publishes a directory of all VORP programs in the United States and overseas.

Victim-Offender Reconciliation Program (VORP)
254 Morgan Blvd.
Valparaiso, IN 46383
(219) 462-1127

10

VOLUNTEER TO PREVENT CRIME

The best thing you can do to prevent crime in your community is to volunteer to organize a meeting between you and your neighbors and your local police. Your police department will know best what the specific dangers are in your neighborhood and what you, as a citizen, can do to prevent criminal activity. In addition, all police departments have outreach workers, usually seasoned cops, who are trained to provide community education—to teach citizens how to protect themselves, their loved ones, their homes, and their possessions.

Here is a checklist of some other things you can do to prevent crime in your neighborhood:

- Put Operation ID stickers on houses throughout your neighborhood, which alert potential robbers that all household valuables are marked with Operation ID engraving pens and can be easily traced. (Your police department can tell you more about this program.)
- Form a neighborhood council or block association to organize anticrime efforts.
- Share phone numbers with neighbors so that you can let each other know if something suspicious is going on.
- Patrol your neighborhood at night in groups, using two-way radios. However, don't confront suspects directly. Call the police if you see anything suspicious.
- Arrange for crime prevention programs to be put on by your local police department.
- Volunteer to help out at your local police station.

- Become a Reserve Corps Officer for your police department. In this job you patrol neighborhoods and help on special days such as the Fourth of July to prevent crime.
- Organize an escort program for anyone who needs help when going out, day or night.
- Ask your local government officials to put in street lamps wherever there are poorly lit areas that make crime easier for perpetrators.
- Publicize your crime prevention efforts to discourage criminals from coming into your area. Criminals will avoid heavily patrolled areas.

The following list provides national resources for volunteering to prevent crime.

American Association of Retired Persons (AARP) Criminal Justice Services

AARP's Criminal Justice Services is a valuable resource for older volunteers working to prevent crime. They will provide your crime prevention group with publications and videos on such issues as how to spot con artists and prevent fraud.

American Association of Retired Persons
Criminal Justice Services
601 E St. NW
Washington, DC 20049
(202) 434-2222

Citizen's Committee for New York City

This association is very strong. It works with more than 10,000 neighborhood associations to prevent crime and stop drugs. This is a great place to get ideas to adapt to your neighborhood.

Citizen's Committee for New York City
305 Seventh Ave.
New York, NY 10001
(212) 989-0909

National Association of Town Watch

This organization sponsors the National Night Out crime prevention event in communities across the country. National Nights Out are held on the first Tuesday in August and reflect the needs of local communities. Activities include crime prevention programs and block parties to increase community spirit. To register your volunteer group contact:

National Association of Town Watch
7 Wynnewood Rd., Suite 215
Wynnewood, PA 19096
(610) 649-7055
(800) 648-3688

National Council on Crime and Delinquency (NCCD)

NCCD is dedicated to crime prevention. Among other things, the council provides prevention programs in public schools and operates programs to combat crime. Contact them at:

National Council on Crime and Delinquency
685 Market St., Suite 620
San Francisco, CA 94105
(415) 896-6223

National Crime Prevention Council (NCPC)

NCPC helps people who want to end crime in their neighborhoods. NCPC provides training and will provide you with ideas about what other communities are doing to prevent crime.

National Crime Prevention Council
1700 K St. NW, 2nd Floor
Washington, DC 20006-3817
(202) 466-NCPC

National Training and Information Center (NTIC)

NTIC supplies community groups with materials on how to organize to fight crime and drugs.

National Training and Information Center
810 North Milwaukee Ave.
Chicago, IL 60622
(312) 243-3035

Triad Programs

Local Triad programs are coalitions of sheriffs, police chiefs, and retired citizens who work together to reduce crime against older people. There are about 100 Triad programs across the country. The Triad's Senior and Lawmen Together (SALT) Council consists of retired persons and law enforcement officers who serve as an advisory group.

Triad Programs
National Sheriff's Association
1450 Duke St.
Alexandria, VA 22314
(703) 836-7827

11

VOLUNTEER IN LIBRARIES OR TEACH ADULTS TO READ

This key covers two important volunteer opportunities: working to strengthen your local library system and teaching adults to read.

Libraries

A strong volunteer group often makes the difference between a sound and creative library system and a mediocre one. You can do many things as a volunteer for your local library system. Most libraries will train you to do your volunteer job efficiently. Some of the activities you could volunteer for are:

- Donate books, and get your neighbors to donate books.
- Sponsor a book drive or organize other fund-raising activities.
- Organize events, lectures, or book clubs.
- Shelve returned books.
- Call library patrons to let them know that the books, audiotapes, or videos that they have requested are available.
- Help repair damaged books.
- Read stories to children or blind people.
- Help drive a bookmobile.

Your public library is not the only place where you can volunteer. Most schools, hospitals and other health institutions, and prisons also have libraries that desperately need volunteers.

If you live in a housing complex or senior housing, or are a member of a social or religious club, you could volunteer to get a committee together to develop a lending library in those locations. If your committee charges cardholders a small daily fee, it will give you income to purchase new books on a regular basis.

The following list provides some national resources for volunteering in libraries.

Friends of Libraries U.S.A. (FOLUSA)

There's a good chance that there is an active Friends of Libraries program in your area supporting your local library. Look in your telephone directory under "Friends of (Your City) Library" to find a program near you.

American Library Association (ALA)

ALA is an association of over 50,000 libraries that uses volunteers in many capacities.

American Library Association
50 E. Huron St.
Chicago, IL 60611
(312) 944-6780
(800) 545-2433

Adult Literacy

About 30 million adults are not able to pick up a newspaper and review the latest news or help their children with their ABCs. They are not able to read. Many pass their illiteracy on to the next generation. If you volunteer for one of the organizations listed below, you will not only be helping adults learn to read, but also their children and their children's children.

You do not need any special skills to teach someone to read, as long as you can read yourself. Most volunteer projects train literacy volunteers.

Here are some resources for volunteering to teach adults to read.

Laubach Literacy Action (LLA)

This is the largest network of volunteer programs on literacy. LLA has over 1,000 programs in 45 states that train volunteers to be tutors to adults and teenagers. If there is not an LLA program in your area, the national office will help you start one.

Laubach Literacy Action
Box 131
1320 Jamesville Ave.
Syracuse, NY 13210
(315) 422-9121

Literacy Volunteers of America (LVA)

There are over 450 programs in the United States run by volunteers who tutor adults. The national office provides help to local literacy programs.

Literacy Volunteers of America
5795 Widewaters Parkway
Syracuse, NY 13214-1846
(315) 445-8000

National Institute for Literacy

This organization's hotline will send you a list of the literacy centers where you can volunteer in your area. The hotline, run by Contact Center Inc., can also provide you with information on how to start a literacy program.

National Literacy Hotline
P.O. Box 81826
Lincoln, NE 68501
(402) 464-0602
(800) 228-8813

Time to Read (TTR)

Time to Read is a volunteer-based literacy program that uses materials donated by Time Inc. magazines. The program can be run through businesses, agencies, prisons, schools, and other entities. Time Warner supplies a trainer for volunteers.

Time to Read
Time Warner Inc.
75 Rockefeller Plaza
New York, NY 10019
(212) 484-8000

12

HELP OUT IN SCHOOLS OR TUTOR STUDENTS

There are many ways to help out the students in your local school system. Here are some ideas:

- Tutor students who need help in specific areas such as languages, math, or the arts.
- Help teachers with supervision during recess, lunchtime, or special events.
- Help direct traffic when needed.
- Become a mentor who provides encouragement and guidance to a young person in need.
- Help with clerical work such as calling families of children who are absent from school, answering phones, or helping out in the library.
- Help provide activities and supervision for latchkey kids who do not have an adult at home to supervise them when school lets out at the end of the day.
- Run book sales, gather donated books, run bake sales, or organize other moneymaking events.
- Get businesses to donate needed items such as sports uniforms, musical instruments, or computer equipment.
- Help keep playgrounds, the school yard, and the general area clean to instill pride in the students.
- If you have a special skill such as carpentry, mechanics, or playing a musical instrument, volunteer to teach students who are interested in learning these skills.

Contact your local school system to find out what programs they have available to train and supervise volunteers, or if you are interested in working on a particular topic, such as helping out in an art class or with auto mechanics, you might contact those teachers directly.

You also might want to look into one of these national organizations.

A Better Chance

A Better Chance places minority students in college preparatory schools.

A Better Chance
419 Boylston St.
Boston, MA 02116-3314
(617) 421-0950

American Association for the
Advancement of Science (AAAS)

AAAS has several strong volunteer programs for active and retired scientists and engineers. The program featured here is the Science and Technology Centers Project (STCP). For information about the others, contact the national office.

STCP involves volunteering in museums around the country. As an STCP volunteer you might serve as a mentor to high school students working on science projects, run a science workshop, organize exhibits, or carry out a range of similar educational projects.

American Association for the Advancement of Science
1333 H St. NW
Washington, DC 20005-4792
(202) 326-6400

Aspira

Aspira helps Latino youth through mentoring programs, career guidance, and club activities. The organization's name comes from the Spanish verb *aspirar,* which means to aspire to something greater.

Aspira
1444 I St. NW, Suite 800
Washington, DC 20005
(202) 835-3600

Cities in Schools (CIS)
This organization works to prevent kids from dropping out
of school. It has programs throughout the United States.

Cities in Schools
1199 North Fairfax St., Suite 300
Alexandria, VA 22314-1436
(703) 519-8999

Help One Student to Succeed (HOSTS)
This highly successful mentoring program for children
and teenagers in grades K through 12 helps students
improve reading and related skills. HOSTS operates over
400 mentoring programs in the United States. Call their
toll free number to find out if there is a program near you:

Help One Student to Succeed
8000 N.E. Parkway Drive, Suite 201
Vancouver, WA 98662
(206) 260-1995
(800) 833-4678

"I Have a Dream" (IHAD) Foundation
IHAD programs "adopt" classes from inner-city schools
or children of the same age who live in public housing
complexes. Volunteers give the children in the group
guidance and tutoring with the goal of keeping them in
school to earn their diplomas. IHAD also provides help
with college tuition for those students who graduate from
high school. Check your local telephone book to see if
there is a program near you.

"I Have a Dream" Foundation
420 W. 26th St.
New York, NY 10001
(212) 229-5844

Junior Achievement

Junior Achievement volunteers with business experience go into public schools to encourage students to do well academically and stay in school to graduate. Call the Junior Achievement toll free number to see if there is a program near you:

Junior Achievement
One Education Way
Colorado Springs, CO 80906
(719) 540-8000
(800) 843-6395

Keep the Promise

Keep the Promise is a five-year campaign to raise awareness of the importance of education and is a collaborative effort of the Business Roundtable, the U.S. Department of Education, the National Governors' Association, the American Federation of Teachers, and the National Alliance of Business. The campaign was started in 1992. One of its goals is to achieve full literacy for all adults. Call the campaign's toll free number, (800) 967-7664, to find out how you can volunteer.

National Association of Partners in Education (NAPE)

NAPE represents over 2.6 million school volunteers. Its clearinghouse can send you information on school volunteer projects. For a small membership fee, NAPE volunteers receive a valuable quarterly newsletter, *School Volunteering*.

National Association of Partners in Education
209 Madison St., Suite 401
Alexandria, VA 22314
(703) 836-4880

Project Excel
National Council of La Raza

Project Excel stands for Excellence in Community Education. Its goal is to improve Hispanic education achievement. Community-based Hispanic organizations sponsor the program, and volunteers are often key to the success of the project.

Project Excel
National Council of La Raza
1111 19th St. NW, Suite 300
Washington, DC 20036
(202) 785-1670

Science By Mail

This innovative mentor program matches children in grades 4 to 9 with volunteer scientists who correspond on specific science projects through the mail. The program is sponsored through Boston's Museum of Science. The program involves 2,500 volunteer scientists. Call their toll free number to find out how to become a volunteer:

Science By Mail
Museum of Science
Science Park
Boston, MA 02114
(617) 589-0437
(800) 729-3300

WAVE (Work, Achievement, Values, and Education) Inc.

WAVE volunteers work with youth to keep them from dropping out of school. WAVE has programs throughout the United States.

WAVE
501 School St. SW, Suite 600
Washington, DC 20024-2754
(202) 484-0103

13

VOLUNTEER FOR ART AND CULTURAL PROGRAMS, PUBLIC RADIO AND TV STATIONS

This key covers two volunteer opportunities important to the cultural enrichment of our communities: art and cultural programs (such as museums and symphonies) and public radio and TV.

Art and Cultural Programs

Art and cultural programs rely heavily on volunteers to function on a daily basis and to put on special events. If you have an interest in the arts, there are many options for helping out, ranging from conducting tours in museums to dancing in a ballet troupe. Most local programs are widely publicized; you may already be aware of the opportunities in your area. For example, there are arts agencies in over 3,000 communities across the United States. They are valuable resources for anyone looking for volunteer opportunities in the arts. If you would like more information about local volunteer opportunities, contact the national organization listed below that addresses your particular interest.

American Association for Museum Volunteers

This association promotes professional standards for museum volunteers.

American Association of Museum Volunteers
1225 I St. NW, Suite 200
Washington, DC 20005
(202) 289-6575

American Symphony Orchestra League

The goal of the League is to strengthen symphony and chamber orchestras. There are 900 member orchestras in the United States.

American Symphony Orchestra League
777 14th St., Suite 500
Washington, DC 20005
(202) 776-0212

Business Volunteers for the Arts (BVAs)

Many cities have BVA chapters through which business people donate their expertise to the arts. Examples of activities that volunteers donate are management skills, finances, fund-raising, and public relations. Check your telephone book to see if there is a BVA listed near you, or contact:

Business Volunteers for the Arts
Arts and Business Council
25 West 45th St., Suite 707
New York, NY 10036-4902
(212) 819-9287, ext. 23

National Assembly of Local Arts Agencies (NALAA)

The goal of this organization is to promote local arts programs. They can guide you to the arts agency near you.

National Assembly of Local Arts Agencies
927 15th St. NW, 12th Floor
Washington, DC 20005
(202) 371-2830

National Assembly of State Arts Agencies
The assembly can guide you to the arts agency in your state

National Assembly of State Arts Agencies
1010 Vermont Ave. NW, Suite 920
Washington, DC 20005
(202) 347-6352

Public Radio and TV
With cutbacks in federal funding constantly threatened, volunteer efforts on behalf of public radio and TV are sorely needed. Contact your local station or:

National Friends of Public Broadcasting (NFPB)
NFPB is a resource for volunteers in public broadcasting. Outstanding volunteers receive recognition at the annual conference, a forum for sharing ideas and receiving training.

National Friends of Public Broadcasting
WFYI
1401 N. Meridian St.
Indianapolis, IN 46202
(317) 636-2020

National Public Radio (NPR)
NPR's membership consists of public radio stations that put programming on free of advertising. Volunteer activities can range from fund-raising to helping broadcast programs.

National Public Radio
635 Massachusetts Ave. NW
Washington, DC 20001-3753
(202) 414-2000

14

WORK TO PRESERVE HISTORIC SITES

When you volunteer to preserve historical sites you are donating your time to safeguard the symbols of our country's past. The following list is a small sample of the large range of organizations working in historic preservation that welcome volunteers. Whether your interest is in saving covered bridges or preserving old military installations, there is a good chance that there is an organization that addresses your particular concern. You will find many other historic preservation organizations listed under the area of your interest in the *Encyclopedia of Associations,* published by Gale Research Inc., and available in most libraries.

American Institute for Conservation of Historic and Artistic Works (AIC)

AIC advances the practice and promotes the importance of the preservation of cultural property.

American Institute for Conservation
of Historic and Artistic Works
1717 K St. NW, Suite 301
Washington, DC 20006
(202) 452-9545

Association of American Historic Inns (AAHI)

AAHI encourages the preservation of historic homes by converting them into inns.

Association of American Historic Inns
P.O. Box 336
Dana Point, CA 92629
(714) 499-8070

Association for Gravestone Studies (AGS)

AGS seeks to promote public awareness of and education about the preservation of gravestones. The association aids community restoration programs.

Association for Gravestone Studies
30 Elm St.
Worcester, MA 01609
(508) 831-7753

Association for the Preservation of Civil War Sites (APCWS)

APCWS fosters interest in the preservation of Civil War sites.

Association for the Preservation of Civil War Sites
613 Caroline St., Suite B
Fredericksburg, VA 22401
(703) 371-1860

Association for Preservation Technology International (APTI)

APTI has many missions in the area of historic preservation including promoting improved quality in the field of historic preservation worldwide, promoting research and gathering technical information on all aspects of historic preservation, and encouraging the establishment of national and local collections of reference materials, tools, and artifacts for study purposes.

Association for Preservation Technology International
P.O. Box 8178
Fredericksburg, VA 22404
(703) 373-1621

Council on America's Military Past (CAMP)

CAMP represents individuals and groups interested in the identification, location, restoration, preservation, and memorialization of old military installations and units. The organization has 20 local groups across the country and publishes the *Journal of America's Military Past*, a quarterly periodical with articles on American military history.

Council on America's Military Past
P.O. Box 1151
Fort Meyer, VA 22211
(703) 379-2006

Great Lakes Lighthouse Keepers Association (GLLKA)

GLLKA represents anyone interested in the historic preservation and restoration of lighthouses on the Great Lakes.

Great Lakes Lighthouse Keepers Association
P.O. Box 580
Allen Park, MI 48101
(313) 426-4150

Heritage Institute of Ellis Island

The institute seeks to foster and promote public awareness of Ellis Island, which served as the entrance point to the United States for 12 million immigrants from 1892 to 1954.

Heritage Institute of Ellis Island
19 E. 48th St., Suite 503
New York, NY 10017
(212) 308-9580

Mount Rushmore Society (MR)

MR is dedicated to preserving Mount Rushmore national monument. It operates in cooperation with the National Park Service.

Mount Rushmore Society
P.O. Box 1524
Rapid City, SD 57709
(605) 341-8883

National Council of Preservation Executives (NCOPE)

NCOPE is the association of executives of nonprofit preservation organizations. It promotes historic preservation through education and public awareness. It operates a clearinghouse and monitors historic preservation legislation.

National Council of Preservation Executives
c/o North Carolina State Historic Preservation Office
109 E. Jones St.
Raleigh, NC 27601-2807
(919) 733-4763

National Trust for Historic Preservation (NTHP)

This private organization was chartered by the U.S. Congress to promote public participation in the preservation of buildings, sites, and objects significant in American history and culture. It gives direct assistance to preservation projects in the form of low-interest loans, matching grants, and expert counsel. NTHP operates as a clearinghouse for information on state, local, federal, and private preservation programs. NTHP publishes *Historic*

Preservation, a bimonthly magazine, which includes articles on the people and organizations working in the field.

National Trust for Historic Preservation
1785 Massachusetts Ave. NW
Washington, DC 20036
(202) 673-4000

Preserve Our Presidential Sites (POPS)

POPS seeks to promote, preserve, and upgrade the grave sites of the 35 deceased American presidents, and educate youth concerning their American heritage and history.

Preserve Our Presidential Sites
201 Bernhardt Dr.
Buffalo, NY 14226-4450
(716) 839-4494

Shenandoah National History Association (SNHA)

SNHA is a group of individuals devoted to maintaining the beauty and history of the Shenandoah National Park in Virginia. They further their cause through the sale of educational materials.

Shenandoah National History Association
Route 4, Box 348
Luray, VA 22835
(703) 999-3581

Society for the Preservation of
New England Antiquities (SPNEA)

This society works to preserve and conserve historic properties and collections. SPNEA promotes the preservation and restoration of architectural landmarks in New England and the interpretation of the region's cultural heritage. The society has a conservation center that researches and develops techniques on architectural conservation, supervises restoration projects, and preserves buildings, fabric, architectural elements, and fine antique furniture. It includes six state groups, owns 44 historic properties, and operates 22 of them as museums. SPNEA has a number of publications, including *SPNEA News,* a quarterly newsletter that reports on SPNEA historic conservation and preservation projects and provides updates on historic properties owned by the society.

Society for the Preservation
  of New England Antiquities
141 Cambridge St.
Boston, MA 02114
(617) 227-3956

Society for the Preservation of Old Mills (SPOOM)

SPOOM works to promote interest, both public and private, in old mills and other Americana passing from the American scene. The society compiles a list of old mills still standing and of those still grinding specialty flour.

Society for the Preservation of Old Mills
c/o William Rigler
Ledford Mill
Route 2, Box 152
Wartrace, TN 37183
(615) 455-2546

2-Lane America

2-Lane America supports the rediscovery of the romance and adventure of open-road touring through the preservation and restoration of rapidly vanishing, historically significant icons of American two-lane highway culture, including scenic byways, mom and pop stores, diners, and roadside curiosities. 2-Lane America is affiliated with the U.S. Route 66 Association in Oxnard, California, which led a successful movement to preserve and revitalize old Route 66.

2-Lane America
P.O. Drawer 5323
Oxnard, CA 93030
(805) 650-0940

Victorian Homeowner's Association and Old House Lovers

The Victorian Homeowner's Association promotes the rehabilitation, historical documentation, and exchange of information on Victorian homes. The association publishes the *Victorian Homeowner's and Old House Lover's Newsletter.*

Victorian Homeowner's Association
  and Old House Lovers
P.O. Box 846
Sutter Creek, CA 95685

Walden Woods Project (WWP)

This organization works to protect two historical land tracts surrounding Walden Pond in Concord, Massachusetts, where Henry Thoreau retreated during the writing of *On Walden Pond.*

Walden Ponds Project
18 Tremont St., Suite 522
Boston, MA 02108
(617) 367-3787

15

HELP PROTECT THE ENVIRONMENT AND WILDLIFE

The opportunities for putting your efforts into environmental action are endless. The enormous number of international, national, and local environmental organizations working in such areas as conserving wildlife, protecting ecosystems, preserving natural forests, and removing toxic wastes makes it impossible to list them all here. Therefore, this key covers but a sampling of the major organizations working to save the globe.

American Littoral Society (ALS)

ALS works to promote the study and conservation of marine life and coastal areas. Among other things, volunteers monitor beaches and water for pollutants. ALS also has the largest catch-and-release sport fishing program in the United States.

American Littoral Society
Baykeeper Volunteer Citizen Water Quality
  Monitoring Project
Sandy Hook
Highlands, NJ 07732
(908) 291-0055

Appalachian Mountain Club (AMC)

AMC sponsors the Volunteer Trails Program through which volunteers maintain 1,400 miles of trails in the Northeast and other areas.

AMC Volunteer Trails Program
5 Joy St.
Boston, MA 02108
(617) 523-0636

Earth First! (EF)

Many consider Earth First! to be a radical environmental group. Some of the organization's goals are to preserve all wilderness areas and recreate those that have been damaged by modern society.

Earth First!
P.O. Box 5176
Missoula, MT 59806

Earthwatch

Through Earthwatch, volunteers pay to travel and conduct scientific research in countries around the world. Projects run from two to three weeks and the cost is tax deductible.

Earthwatch
680 Mt. Auburn St.
Box 403
Watertown, MA 02272
(800) 776-0188

Environmental Alliance for Senior Involvement (EASI)

EASI, a program of the Alliance for Environmental Education, brings together groups of older people, environmental organizations, and volunteer agencies who are working on environmental issues.

Environmental Alliance for Senior Involvement
8733 Old Dumphries Rd.
Katlett, VA 22019
(540) 788-3274

National Audubon Society

The National Audubon Society works to protect wildlife and wildlife habitats. One of their major priorities is restoring the natural balance critical to life. The society has a wide range of programs including studying wildlife and ecosystems, maintaining sanctuaries established by the Society, lobbying to protect the environment, litigating to protect endangered species, grassroots organizing, and public education.

Audubon has 500 volunteer chapters, which address local conservation issues. The society publishes *Audubon* magazine bimonthly.

National Audubon Society
700 Broadway
New York, NY 10003-9501
(212) 979-3000

The Nature Conservancy (TNC)

TNC is committed to finding, purchasing, protecting, and maintaining natural habitats for rare species throughout the world. The Conservancy owns and manages 1,300 natural preserves. Volunteers perform most of the activities of conservation and restoration.

The Nature Conservancy
1815 N. Lynn St.
Arlington, VA 22209
(703) 841-5300

Rails-to-Trails Conservancy (RTC)

This organization works to convert railroad tracks and corridors that are not in use into trails for public uses such as cross-country skiing and walking. Volunteers help maintain the trails.

Rails-to-Trails Conservancy
1400 16th St. NW, Suite 300
Washington, DC 20036
(202) 797-5400

Rainforest Action Network (RAN)

RAN works to save the world's tropical rain forests and the rights of those living near them. RAN has 150 Rainforest Association Groups (RAGs) in the United States and Europe, all of which rely heavily on volunteers.

Rainforest Action Network
450 Sansome St.
San Francisco, CA 94111
(415) 398-4404

Sierra Club (SC)

The Sierra Club is dedicated to stopping abuse of irreplaceable wilderness lands, to saving endangered species, and to protecting the global environment. Its conservation activities include creating and enlarging national parks, designating wilderness areas, preserving forests, halting dams and off-shore drilling, lobbying for sensible energy policies, and working to prevent destruction of natural habitats. The Sierra Club has 61 chapters that offer conservation activities.

Sierra Club
730 Polk St.
San Francisco, CA 94109
(415) 776-2211

U.S. Department of Agriculture
Forest Service

The Forest Service uses over 70,000 volunteers every year to work in the 156 national forests and 19 national grasslands that it manages. Volunteer activities range from physical work such as maintaining trails to taking photographs and conducting research. All volunteers receive training. Contact one of the regional Forest Service offices in Juneau, Alaska; Milwaukee, Wisconsin; Ogden, Utah; Missoula, Montana; Portland, Oregon; San Francisco, California; Lakewood, Colorado; Atlanta, Georgia; or Albuquerque, New Mexico, or the national office:

Forest Service, U.S. Department of Agriculture
Human Resources Dept.
12th St. and Independence Ave. SW
P.O. Box 96090
Washington, DC 20090-6090
(202) 205-1760

U.S. Department of the Interior
Volunteers in Parks (VIP)

The VIP program has over 22,000 volunteers who work in U.S. parks. Volunteer activities range from maintaining campsites to planting trees. Contact one of the Department of Interior regional offices in Anchorage, Alaska; Philadelphia, Pennsylvania; Omaha, Nebraska; Boston, Massachusetts; Washington, DC; Seattle, Washington; Denver, Colorado; Atlanta, Georgia; Santa Fe, New Mexico; San Francisco, California, or the national office:

U.S. Department of the Interior
Volunteers in Parks
1849 C St. NW
Washington, DC 20240
(202) 208-3100

U.S. Fish and Wildlife Service Office

There are over 500 national wildlife refuges on 90 million acres in the United States where your volunteer services are welcome These refuges are home to more than 60 endangered species, and the work of volunteers is important to their survival. To learn about the opportunities in your area, contact the volunteer coordinator at the closest regional office, listed under U.S. Fish and Wildlife Service Office in the government section in the telephone directory for the following cities: Anchorage, Alaska; Hadley, Massachusetts; Fort Snelling, Minnesota; Portland, Oregon; Denver, Colorado; Atlanta, Georgia; and Albuquerque, New Mexico.

The Wilderness Society

The Wilderness Society works toward the long-term protection of public lands and wildlife. Among many other achievements, it has helped to pass wilderness bills in 44 states. There are ten field offices in the United States that welcome volunteers.

The Wilderness Society
900 17th St. NW
Washington, DC 20006
(202) 833-2300

Other National Programs to Consider

Contact these organizations to locate an affiliate near you:

Clean Water
Clean Water Action, 1320 18th St. NW, Suite 300, Washington, DC 20036, (202) 457-1286

Endangered Species
The Xerxes Society, 4828 SE Hawthorne Blvd., Portland, OR 97215

Energy Conservation
Energy Efficiency and Renewable Energy Clearinghouse, P.O. Box 3048, Merrifield, VA 22116, (800) 523-2929

Environmental Education
The Natural Guard, 2631 Durham Rd., North Guilford, CT 06437, (203) 457-1302

General Environmental and Conservation Issues
Environmental Defense Fund (EDF), 257 Park Ave. South, New York, NY 10010, (212) 505-2100
Friends of the Earth, 1025 Vermont Ave. NW, Suite 300, Washington, DC 20005, (202) 783-7400
Greenpeace, 1436 U St. NW, Washington, DC 20009, (202) 462-1177
Izaak Walton League of America, 14708 Mt. Olive Rd., Centreville, VA 22020, (703) 528-1818
League of Conservation Voters (LCV), 1707 L St. NW, Suite 550, Washington, DC 20036, (202) 785-VOTE
Natural Resources Defense Council (NRDC), 40 West 20th St., New York, NY 10011, (212) 727-2700
Renew America, 1400 16th St. NW, Suite 710, Washington, DC 20036, (202) 232-2252

Global Management
Windstar Foundation, 2317 Snowmass Creek Road, Snowmass, CO 81654, (970) 927-4777
Worldwatch, 1776 Massachusetts Ave. NW, Washington, DC 20036, (202) 452-1999

Greenhouse Effect
The Greenhouse Crisis Foundation, 1660 L St. NW, Suite 630, Washington, DC 20036, (202) 466-2823

Hazardous/Toxic Waste
Citizen's Clearinghouse for Hazardous Waste (CCHW), P.O. Box 6806, Falls Church, VA 22040, (703) 237-CCHW

National Parks
National Parks and Conservation Association (NPCA), 1776 Massachusetts Ave. NW, Suite 200, Washington, DC 20036, (202) 223-6722

Population Growth
Zero Population Growth, 1400 16th St. NW, Suite 320, Washington, DC 20036, (202) 332-2200

Rain Forests
Conservation International (CI), 1015 18th St. NW, Suite 1000, Washington, DC 20036, (202) 429-5660
Rainforest Alliance, 65 Bleecker St., New York, NY 10012-2420, (212) 677-1900

Recycling
National Recycling Coalition Inc., 1101 30th St. NW, Suite 305, Washington, DC 20036, (202) 797-6800

Wildlife
Defenders of Wildlife, 1101 14th St. NW, Suite 1400, Washington, DC 20005, (202) 682-9400
National Wildlife Federation (NWF), 1400 16th St. NW, Washington, DC 20036, (202) 797-6800
World Wildlife Fund (WWF), 1250 24th St. NW, Washington, DC 20037, (202) 293-4800

16

WORK WITH ANIMALS

If you like to work with animals, you have a wide range of options available to you. For example, you could cheer up nursing home residents by visiting them with your dog or other pet, or you could volunteer to take care of the pets of people who have AIDS or other limiting and life-threatening illnesses. You also could take part in wildlife population counts, train guide dogs for the blind, work to save your favorite endangered species, or take care of injured wildlife.

The following list is a cross section of volunteer opportunities available for working with animals. Animal rights organizations appear at the end of the list.

National Audubon Society
Christmas Bird Count

The Christmas Bird Count is a bird census that takes place annually. Over 40,000 volunteers participate in and outside of the United States. NAS prefers that you write them at the following address rather than call for information:

Christmas Bird Count
National Audubon Society
700 Broadway
New York, NY 10003

Cornell Laboratory of Ornithology (CLO)

CLO has a number of bird population studies that are ongoing and that take place throughout the United States. For example, in Project Feederwatch, volunteers track bird populations at backyard feeders during certain periods of the year.

Cornell Laboratory of Ornithology
Bird Research
159 Sapsucker Woods Road
Ithaca, NY 14850
(607) 254-BIRD

Guide Dog Foundation for the Blind Inc. (GDF)
Puppy Walkers Program

The Guide Dog Foundation provides trained dogs to the blind. If you volunteer as a GDF puppy walker, a golden or Labrador retriever will spend a year with you learning to go everywhere sighted people go. GDF has projects in New York and other states. Call their toll free number to find a program near you:

Guide Dog Foundation for the Blind Inc.
Puppy Walkers Program
371 East Jericho Tpke.
Smithtown, NY 11787
(516) 265-2121
(800) 548-4337

Guided Eyes for the Blind Inc. (GEB)
Puppy Raising Program

If you become a volunteer puppy raiser for GEB, you will have a guide-dog-in-training living with you for about 14 months. During that time you will spend a couple of hours every day with the dog, teaching it how to aid the blind. GEB has projects in eight states. Call their toll free number to find a program near you:

Guided Eyes for the Blind Inc.
Puppy Raising Program
611 Granite Springs Heights Road
Yorktown Heights, NY 01598
(914) 878-3330 (in Patterson, NY)
(800) 942-0149

The International Wildlife Rehabilitation Council (IWRC)

IWRC distributes information about wildlife rehabilitation centers around the world, which provide care to wildlife that are sick, injured, or orphaned.

The International Wildlife Rehabilitation Council
4437 Central Place, Suite B-4
Suisan, CA 94585
(707) 864-1761

Delta Society (DS)

The Delta Society focuses on the well-being created by relationships between animals and people. Among other things, it is a clearinghouse for dogs trained to help people with disabilities. DS has a number of popular programs, including the Pet Partners program listed here. They also have a database of people and pet projects across the country. Call one of their toll free numbers to find out about other DS programs:

The Delta Society
289 Perimeter Road East
Renton, WA 98055-1329
(206) 226-7357
(800) 869-6898 or
(800) 809-2714 (voice/TDD)

The National Wildlife Rehabilitators Association (NWRA)

NWRA is an association of veterinarians and others who provide care for animals in wildlife centers around the country. They can provide you with information about the wildlife center closest to you where you can volunteer your time.

The National Wildlife Rehabilitators Association
14 North Seventh Ave.
St. Cloud, MN 56303
(612) 259-4086

Pacific Whale Foundation (PWF)

PWF works to preserve oceans and save marine animals. They offer internships in areas such as Hawaii and Australia. Call their toll free number for information on volunteering:

Pacific Whale Foundation
101 N. Kihei Road
Kihei, HI 96753
(808) 879-8860
(800) WHALE11

Pet Partners Program

This program brings volunteers and their pets to people in nursing homes and elderly people who live alone. Training is provided. The Pets Partners Program is run by the Delta Society. Call one of their toll free numbers to see if there is a program near you:

The Delta Society
289 Perimeter Road East
Renton, WA 98055-1329
(206) 226-7357
(800) 869-6898 or
(800) 809-2714 (voice/TDD)

Pets Are Wonderful Support (PAW)

This San Francisco-based program was the first in the country to help pet owners who are infected with AIDS. There are now many similar programs across the country (look in your local telephone directory under pets or AIDS, or call the toll free AIDS hotline, (800) 342-2437.

71

Pets Are Wonderful Support
539 Castro St.
San Francisco, CA 94114
(415) 241-1460

U.S. Department of the Interior
Fish and Wildlife Service (FWS)

Volunteers for the Fish and Wildlife Service perform tasks such as taking wildlife population counts at national refuges and fish hatcheries. Contact the national office for the location of a regional office close to you, and to request information on volunteering.

U.S. Department of the Interior
Fish and Wildlife Service
Interior Building
18th and C Sts. NW
Washington, DC 20240
(202) 208-5634

Animal Rights Organizations

Animal rights organizations work for the humane treatment of animals.

American Humane Association (AHA)

The American Humane Association is the oldest national animal rights organization in the country. Their focus ranges from emergency animal relief to publications for pet owners. Call their toll free number to learn more about AHA programs and activities in your area:

American Humane Association
63 Inverness Drive E
Englewood, CO 80112-5117
(303) 792-9900
(800) 227-4645

Animal Protection Institute (API)

API's goal is to stop and prevent the abuse of all animals—whether they be pets, farm animals, or wildlife. Call their toll free number to find out how you can help:

Animal Protection Institute
2831 Fruitridge Road
Sacramento, CA 95820
(916) 731-5521
(800) 348-7387

Animal Rights Mobilization (ARM!)

ARM! is a grassroots organization that works to end the consumption of animals as food, for hunting, for their fur, and in laboratory research. ARM! has affiliated groups all across the country. Call their toll free number to learn more about their programs and find the organization closest to you:

Animal Rights Mobilization
234 Columbine St.
Denver, CO 80206
(303) 388-7120
(800) CALL ARM

Farm Animal Reform Movement (FARM)

FARM works to prevent animal agriculture. Two popular FARM programs are the Great American Meatout and World Farm Animals Day, which FARM sponsors annually. Call their toll free number to learn more about their programs and to find out if there is an affiliate near you:

Farm Animal Reform Movement
P.O. Box 30654
Bethesda, MD 20824
(301) 530-1737
(800) MEATOUT

Friends of Animals (FOA)

FOA is an animal protection organization with an international focus. Among other things, volunteers are encouraged to work for legislation that prevents animal abuse. FOA suggests that volunteers send news clippings about animal protection issues or abuse to the national office. For information about FOA's extensive programs call their toll free number:

Friends of Animals
777 Post Road, Suite 205
Darien, CT 06820
(203) 656-1522
(800) 321-PETS

In Defense of Animals (IDA)

IDA is a large membership organization that works to defend the rights, welfare, and habitat of animals. They sponsor a number of programs including World Laboratory Animal Liberation Week, anti-fur demonstrations, boycotts, and lobbying to stop the killing of seals. IDA has a database of volunteers throughout the country. To contact IDA's stolen pet hotline, call their toll free number. For information about IDA programs, call or write to them at:

In Defense of Animals
131 Camino Alto, Suite E
Mill Valley, CA 94941
(415) 388-9641
IDA Stolen Pet Hotline
(800) STOLENPET

People for the Ethical Treatment of Animals (PETA)

PETA is an activist organization that works to prevent animal abuses. PETA has a computerized database of animal rights groups throughout the country. Call their action line for a recording of activities you can take part in:

People for the Ethical Treatment of Animals
P.O. Box 42516
Washington, DC 20015
(301) 770-PETA
Action Line: (301) 770-8980

Sea Shepherd Conservation Society (SSCS)
This activist organization works to assure the enforcement of international treaties for the conservation of ocean animals such as seals, whales, and dolphins. Volunteers work as crew members in ocean patrols.

Sea Shepherd Conservation Society
P.O. Box 628
Venice, CA 90294
(310) 301-SEAL

17

VOLUNTEER WITH CHILDREN AND TEENS

There are many ways to pass the wisdom of your years down to children and adolescents. You could volunteer for an agency such as the highly successful Foster Grandparent program (see page 15) or Family Friends Programs (see page 119 to 120). You could help out latchkey children in your neighborhood who need the attention of an adult after school hours. Or you could volunteer at your closest children's hospital, children's museum, or public school.

The following listings show the tremendous range of options that are open to you if you would like to volunteer your time with youth.

Big Brothers/Big Sisters of America

If you become a big brother or big sister you will serve as a role model to an at-risk school-age child. This means spending an average of four hours a week one-on-one with your little brother or little sister enjoying activities together such as visiting museums, attending sports events, or sharing an ice cream sundae. The staff of local associations carefully match up the volunteer and child. There are usually long waiting lists of children waiting for volunteers.

There are over 500 affiliated Big Brothers/Big Sisters of America programs in the United States. Look in your local phone book to find an agency near you or contact:

Big Brothers/Big Sisters of America
230 N. 13th St.
Philadelphia, PA 19107
(215) 567-7000

Boy Scouts of America (BSA)

BSA provides educational programs for young people. Boy Scouts focuses on helping boys develop self-reliance, resourcefulness, and a desire to help others. Check your local telephone directory under Boy Scouts for a program near you, or contact:

Boy Scouts of America
1325 W. Walnut Hill Lane
Irving, TX 75015
(214) 580-2000

Camp Fire Boys and Girls

If you volunteer for a Camp Fire program you might help run a club for young people, take members on hikes in the country, or help them run a food drive. Children and youths from infancy to age 21 can be a Camp Fire Boy or Girl. To find a program near you look in your telephone directory or contact:

Camp Fire Boys and Girls
4601 Madison Ave.
Kansas City, MO 64112
(816) 756-1950

Covenant House (CH)

Covenant House serves thousands of runaway kids across the country every year. Volunteers provide food, shelter, clothing, medical care, counseling, vocational training, and more to children who have left home. Its Rights of Passage program helps find jobs for kids, and its hotline, called Nineline, is available around the clock every day of the year for runaways and their families. Call CH's toll free number to find a program near you:

Covenant House
346 West 17th St.
New York, NY 10011-5002
(212) 604-0094
(800) 999-9999

Fresh Air Fund

The fund provides free summer vacations in a northeastern state to disadvantaged children from New York City. Children ages 6 to 18 go to camp or visit families who live in nonurban environments. If you are interested in hosting a child in your home call the Fresh Air Fund's toll free number, or contact:

Fresh Air Fund
1040 Avenue of the Americas, 3rd Floor
New York, New York 10018
(212) 221-0900
(800) 367-0003

Girl Scouts of the United States of America

Your local Girl Scouts council serves girls ages 5 to 17 in troops that provide opportunities for members to develop their potential, make friends, and become members of their communities. As a volunteer you can be a troop leader, drive a car pool, teach a skill, or contribute in a number of other ways. Check your telephone directory under Girl Scouts to find a troop near you.

Girl Scouts of the U.S.A.
420 5th Ave.
New York, NY 10018-2702
(212) 852-8000

Head Start

Head Start is a federally funded program for children ages 3 to 5 from low-income families. Head Start focuses on education, health, parental involvement, and social services. Look in your local telephone directory to find out if there is a Head Start program near you, or contact:

Head Start
Department of Health and Human Services
P.O. Box 1182
Washington, DC 20013
(202) 645-3707

Help One Student to Succeed (HOSTS)

HOSTS is a mentoring program for youth in grades K through 12. Volunteers work with students to improve reading, writing, vocabulary, study skills, and life skills. HOSTS has more than 400 programs in the United States. Look in your phone directory or call HOST's toll free number to find a program near you:

HOSTS Corporation
8000 N.E. Parkway Drive, Suite 201
Vancouver, WA 98662-6459
(360) 260-1995
(800) 833-4678

Linking Lifetimes

Run by the Center for Intergenerational Learning, there are close to ten Linking Lifetimes programs across the country. Volunteer mentors spend two to four hours a week with an at-risk youth. All volunteers receive training and must commit a year to working with the young person. To find a program near you, or to find out how to start a program contact:

Linking Lifetimes
Center for Intergenerational Living
Temple University
1601 N. Broad St., Room 206
Philadelphia, PA 19122
(215) 204-6970

Magic Me

This intergenerational program brings together middle school children and residents of nursing homes. Magic Me programs are starting all over the country. To find a program near you or to find out how to start your own program contact:

Magic Me
2521 N. Charles St.
Baltimore, MD 21218
(410) 243-9066

National Committee to Prevent Child Abuse (NCPCA)

This organization is dedicated to preventing child abuse. NCPCA also sponsors Health Families America, which helps parents get off to a good start to prevent abuse. NCPCA has chapters in all 50 states. Call their toll free number to find a chapter near you or contact:

National Committee to Prevent Child Abuse
  (NCPCA)
332 South Michigan Ave., Suite 1600
Chicago, IL 60604-4357
(312) 663-3520
(800) 55-NCPCA

The National Exchange Club Foundation
for the Prevention of Child Abuse

This organization trains volunteers to work directly with parents to prevent abuse. The foundation has programs throughout the United States. Call the foundation's toll free number to find a program near you, or contact:

The National Exchange Club Foundation for the
  Prevention of Child Abuse
3050 Central Ave.
Toledo, OH 43606
(419) 535-3232
(800) 760-3413

National 4-H Council

4-H volunteers help children and youths age 9 to 19 develop projects in areas such as forestry, gardening, sewing, and cooking. 4-H is active in every county in the United States and is no longer an exclusively rural program. In fact, most participants live in urban or suburban areas. Your closest Cooperative Extension Office, listed in the government section of your phone book, will know about 4-H clubs nearby. Or contact:

National 4-H Council
7100 Connecticut Ave.
Chevy Chase, MD 20815
(301) 961-2800

One to One

There are ten One to One programs in the United States. They provide a structure for volunteers to help at-risk children and youths. One to One also publishes guides on mentoring. Contact the national headquarters to see if there is a program near you:

One to One
2801 M St. NW
Washington, DC 20007
(202) 338-3844

Reading Is Fundamental (RIF)

RIF is a network of more than 152,000 volunteers who work at over 15,000 sites to get children excited about reading. RIF has also started programs to work with older age groups and the homeless. Contact:

Reading Is Fundamental
600 Maryland Ave. SW, Suite 600
Washington, DC 20560
(202) 287-3220

The Vanished Children's Alliance (VCA)

Dedicated to the prevention and recovery of missing children, the alliance helps to find missing children and it networks with other organizations working on similar issues. Call VCA's toll free number to find out how you can volunteer, or contact:

The Vanished Children's Alliance (VCA)
1407 Parkmoore Ave., Suite 200
San Jose, CA 95126
(408) 971-4822
National Sighting Line
(800) VANISHED

Breakthrough for Youth

There are many Breakthrough for Youth programs throughout the United States. Started by the Breakthrough Foundation, the programs emphasize positive behavior and work to improve the quality of life for youth who might otherwise get into trouble. Contact the program's main office to see if there is a program near you:

Breakthrough for Youth
1610 Wynkood St., No. 105
Denver, CO 80202-1135
(303) 575-6746

Other National Programs to Consider

Contact these organizations to locate an affiliate near you:

Missing Children

The Adam Walsh Children's Fund, 9176 Highway A1A Alternate, Suite 200, Lake Park, FL 33404, (407) 863-7900.

Child Find of America, 7 Innis Ave., P.O. Box 277, New Paltz, NY 12561-9277, (914) 255-1848

Find the Children, 11811 West Olympic Blvd., Los Angeles, CA 90064, (800) 843-5678

The Missing Children HELP Center, 410 Ware Blvd., Suite 400, Tampa, FL 33619, (813) 623-KIDS, 24-hour National Hotline (800) USA-KIDS

The National Center for Missing and Exploited Children (NCMEC), 2101 Wilson Blvd., Suite 550, Arlington, VA 22201, (800) 843-5678

Sponsoring Poor Children Throughout the World

Childreach, 155 Plan Way, Warwick, RI 02886, (401) 737-5770, (800) 556-7918

Children Incorporated, P.O. Box 5381, Richmond, VA 23220, (804) 359-4592 (800) 538-5381

The Christian Children's Fund, 2821 Emerywood Parkway, Richmond, VA 23261, (800) 776-6767

Feed the Children, P.O. Box 36, Oklahoma City, OK, 73101-0036, (405) 942-0228

Futures for Children, 9600 Tennyson St. NE, Albuquerque, NM 87122 (800) 545-6843 (for American Indian children)

Pearl S. Buck Foundation, Green Hills Farm, 520 Dublin Rd., Hilltown, Perkasie, PA 18944, (215) 249-0100, (800) 220-BUCK

Save the Children (STC), 54 Wilton Rd., Westport, CT 06880, (203) 221-4000, (800) 243-5075

18

FEED THE HUNGRY; HELP LOW-INCOME AND HOMELESS PEOPLE

This key covers feeding people who are in need of a nutritious meal, and helping out low-income and homeless people.

Feed the Hungry
There are many wonderful programs available where you can volunteer to help people in need of a daily meal. Here are some national resources.

Foodchain—The Association of Prepared and Perishable Food Rescue Programs

Foodchain volunteers rescue unused, edible food—that would otherwise be thrown away—from restaurants and other food suppliers. There are over 100 programs in the United States. The staff of the national headquarters helps volunteers start programs in their communities. Call their toll free number to find out if there is a program near you:

Foodchain—The Association of Prepared
  and Perishable Food Rescue Programs
970 Jefferson St. NW
Atlanta, GA 30318
(404) 875-4322
(800) 845-3008

The Gleaning Network

Gleaning programs collect edible food from farms, orchards, and other places, which would be wasted if it was not gleaned by volunteers. Call The Gleaning Network's toll free number to find out if there is a program in your state or to get information about starting a program in your state:

The Gleaning Network
Society of Saint Andrew
P.O. Box 329
State Route 615
Big Island, VA 24526
(804) 333-4597
(800) 299-5956

The Hope Foundation (THF)
This organization is an information center for volunteers across the country who want to help the homeless. Providing meals is an important part of their services. Call the foundation's toll free number to find out about homeless shelters in your community.

The Hope Foundation
1499 Regal Row, Suite 316
Dallas, TX 75247
(214) 630-5766
(800) 843-4073

Love Is Feeding Everyone (LIFE)
LIFE works to end domestic hunger through collecting and distributing food that would otherwise be thrown away. While their volunteer efforts are centered in Los Angeles, LIFE distributes a training film and manual for those who want to adopt the program in their area.

Love Is Feeding Everyone
310 North Fairfax Ave.
Los Angeles, CA 90036
(213) 936-0895

Meals-on-Wheels

These community programs provide a hot, nutritious meal to elderly people who cannot prepare their own meals. Volunteers are needed to prepare and cook meals, deliver meals, and help out in the offices. Local telephone directories often list phone numbers for local Meals-on-Wheels programs, or your local office on aging will have their phone number (look in your phone book under aging services).

Second Harvest National Food Bank Network

This network of almost 200 food banks is the largest charitable food bank in the United States. Every year more than 500 million pounds of food are distributed through Second Harvest programs. Call their toll free number to find out if there is a food bank near you:

Second Harvest National Food Bank Network
116 South Michigan Ave., 4th Floor
Chicago, IL 60603
(312) 263-2303
(800) 532-FOOD

Share Our Strength (SOS)

SOS provides public education, grant distribution, and community outreach to fight hunger. One well-known benefit run by SOS is the Taste of the Nation, a food and wine tasting event held in communities in the spring, which raises money for relief of hunger. SOS also works to get restaurants to donate leftover food to shelters and food banks. They have a joint program, called the Charge Against Hunger Campaign, run with American Express, which raises funds to fight hunger. Call their toll free number to find out if there is a food bank near you, or contact:

Share Our Strength
1511 K St. NW, Suite 940
Washington, DC 20005
(202) 393-2925
(800) 969-4SOS

USA Harvest

This organization is unusual because it does not accept financial donations. Volunteers donate food, time, transportation, and materials, but not money. For example, as a volunteer you might pick up food at a restaurant and deliver it to a center where people come to eat. Call their toll free number to find out if there is a USA Harvest center near you:

USA Harvest
P.O. Box 1628
Louisville, KY 40201
(800) USA-4-FOOD

World Food Day

This event takes place every year on October 16 in 150 nations across the world. The purpose of World Food Day is to increase awareness about global hunger. Over 450 national organizations, the U.S. Government, and over 20,000 volunteers sponsor World Food Day in the 50 states. For information on volunteering contact:

The U.S. National Committee for World Food Day
1001 22nd St. NW
Washington, DC 20437
(202) 653-2404

Help Low-Income and Homeless People

Here are some national resources for helping low-income and homeless people.

Box Project

The Box Project is dedicated to helping people who live in poverty areas. Volunteers send a box of needed items on a regular basis to a "sister family." Part of the concept behind the program is that volunteers send their friendship as well as food or clothing. Volunteers and sister families check in with one another at least once a month to see how they are doing. The Box Project also sponsors a Holiday Santa project where volunteers send boxes to a needy family at Christmas time.

The Box Project
Box 435
Plainville, CT 06062
(800) 268-9928

The Hope Foundation (THF)

This organization is an information center for volunteers across the country who want to help the homeless. For more information, see page 85.

The International Union of Gospel Missions (IUGM)

This Christian association of more than 200 inner-city rescue missions provides food, shelter, and counseling services to thousands of homeless people. Call IUGM's toll free number to find out about homeless shelters near you, or contact:

The International Union of Gospel Missions (IUGM)
1045 Swift St.
North Kansas City, MO 64116-4127
(816) 471-8020
(800) 624-5156

Traveler's Aid

Traveler's Aid provides emergency relief for the homeless, poor, runaways, victims of abuse, and others who need a safe place to rest. Traveler's Aid also has information and referral desks at airports, train stations, and other transportation points to aid travelers. Traveler's Aid is particularly interested in volunteers who speak foreign languages.

The American Bar Association (ABA)

The ABA's Commission on Homelessness and Poverty provides legal assistance to the homeless. There are 75 programs in the United States. Contact the ABA to find out about programs in your area:

American Bar Association
740 15th St. NW
Washington, DC 20061
(202) 662-1000

The American Institute of Architects and
The American Institute of Architect Students

Volunteer architects assist in designing and constructing facilities for the homeless.

The American Institute of Architects
The American Institute of Architect Students
1735 New York Ave. NW
Washington, DC 20006
(202) 626-7492

19

VOLUNTEER TO HELP THE ELDERLY

The elderly population is diverse. Many elderly people lead active lives and are not in need of help, while others do need assistance with at least some daily tasks such as shopping, bathing, or paying bills. In fact, today about one-quarter of seniors living in the community require some form of help like this. The volunteer activities in this key address these needs.

American Association of Retired Persons (AARP)

AARP's Volunteer Talent Bank matches potential volunteers to opportunities. Examples of the issues you can volunteer for are long-term care policy development, elder abuse prevention, legal assistance for elders, health care policy, fraud and crime prevention, and housing.

Volunteer Talent Bank
AARP Fulfillment
601 E St. NW
Washington, DC 20049
(202) 434-3219

Generations United (GU)

This organization is a good resource for locating volunteer programs that focus on older and younger generations working together.

Generations United
440 First St. NW, Suite 310
Washington, DC 20001-2085
(202) 638-2952

Little Brothers—Friends of the Elderly (LBFE)

LBFE volunteers offer relief from isolation to elderly people who live alone. Volunteers carry out such activities as visiting older people, telephoning them on a regular basis to make sure they are OK, and providing companionship and transportation for them. There are LBFE programs in a number of cities including Chicago, Minneapolis, St. Paul, Boston, Philadelphia, and San Francisco. Contact the main office to see if there is a program near you:

Little Brothers—Friends of the Elderly
1603 South Michigan Ave., Suite 502
Chicago, IL 60616
(312) 786-0501

Meals-on-Wheels

These community programs provide a hot, nutritious meal to elderly people who cannot prepare their own meals. For more information about Meals-on-Wheels see page 86.

Nursing Home Assistance

Most nursing home residents are in great need of companionship and assistance with small tasks like getting to doctor's appointments or writing letters. Often just sitting and talking with a nursing home resident is a welcome remedy for loneliness.

Here are some suggestions for what you could do to cheer up life for nursing home residents:

- Take them to visit friends who may not be able to travel to see them, or bring the friends to them.
- Help write letters to loved ones.
- Read letters, books, magazines, or newspapers to residents who have vision problems.
- Check out library books and tapes and bring them to residents regularly.

- Drive them to appointments or to do errands.
- Organize parties on their birthdays and special holidays.
- Help them write their life histories or create photo albums and scrapbooks to pass down to future generations.
- See that they get to the spiritual/religious services of their choice on a regular basis.
- Brighten up their rooms; take them plants or pictures if appropriate.
- Take them out for walks, to the movies, or for rides in a car.
- Find out what their favorite foods are and cook for them.
- Play cards or favorite games with them.

To locate a nursing home near you, look in your local telephone book under nursing homes.

Prevent Elder Abuse

Every year many defenseless elderly people are abused or have their rights taken away by their caregivers or the staff of the institutions they live in. Many local areas have programs where you can volunteer to be on the lookout and take action against such mistreatment. Three excellent resources are

1. Your Local Office on Aging. This will be listed in your telephone book under such categories as senior services or aging programs. Call and ask what opportunities they have for volunteering to prevent elder abuse.

2. The National Citizen's Coalition for Nursing Home Reform (NCCNHR). This organization was founded to protect and improve the care and quality of life of all nursing home residents. Contact them at: 1224 M St. NW, Suite 301, Washington, DC 20005-5183, (202) 393-2018.

3. Your Long-Term Care Ombudsman. Ombudsmen welcome conscientious volunteers to help them monitor services in long-term care settings. Every state and the District of Columbia have ombudsmen, listed under your state office on aging in your telephone book.

Senior Companion Program (SCP)

SCP is a volunteer program sponsored by the federal government in which older people help others in their age group who are in need of assistance. Senior companions visit the elderly in nursing homes and hospitals, and those who are homebound. As a senior companion, you might shop for your clients, cook or do household chores, or refer them to services they need.

Senior Companions with low incomes can qualify for a stipend funded by the federal government. Look in your local telephone book to find a Senior Companion program in your area, or check with your closest office on aging or area agency on aging. Or contact the following to find out the regional office near you:

The Corporation for National and Community Service
1100 Vermont Ave. NW
Washington, DC 20525
(202) 606-5000

Seniors in Service to Seniors

This program, sponsored by the Points of Light Foundation, encourages older Americans to volunteer by identifying at-risk seniors and helping them get the services they need.

Seniors in Service to Seniors
Points of Light Foundation
1737 H St. NW
Washington, DC 20036
(202) 223-9186

20

VOLUNTEER WITH HEALTH ORGANIZATIONS

The goals of the organizations described below are to improve the health and care of people with specific health problems such as heart disease and arthritis, or, like the American Red Cross, their efforts cover a number of important health issues. Without a strong corps of volunteers these organizations could not carry out the excellent services they provide.

For information on volunteering to help people with AIDS, cancer, blindness, deafness, disabilities, drug or alcohol abuse, or mental health problems see Keys 21 through 26. If you would like to learn how to donate blood or organs see Key 27. To volunteer for hospitals or other health institutions see Key 28.

American Heart Association (AHA)

Heart disease is the leading killer in the United States. AHA's purpose is to reduce the death and disability caused by the disease. Close to 4 million Americans volunteer on the local and national level for the American Heart Association. Call their toll free number to locate the chapter close to you:

American Heart Association
7272 Greenville Ave.
Dallas, TX 75231
(214) 373-6300
(800) AHA-USA1

American Diabetes Association (ADA)

ADA works to prevent and control diabetes, an insulin-related disease that affects nearly 14 million Americans. More than 250,000 people in the United States die of the disease every year. There are about 800 ADA chapters nationwide that welcome volunteers. Look in your local telephone directory under American Diabetes Association or call their toll free number to find a chapter near you:

American Diabetes Association
1660 Duke St.
Alexandria, VA 22314
(703) 549-1500
(800) 232-3472

American Liver Foundation (ALF)

ALF works to prevent hepatitis, liver and gall bladder diseases, and related health problems. There are over 20 chapters across the country. Call the ALF toll free number to find the program near you, or contact:

American Liver Foundation
1425 Pompton Ave.
Cedar Grove, NJ 07009
(201) 256-2550
(800) 223-0179

American Lung Association (ALA)

Founded to fight tuberculosis, ALA now works to prevent and cure all lung diseases. There are about 120 affiliates throughout the United States. Call ALA's toll free number to find the program closest to you or look in your local telephone directory under the American Lung Association.

American Lung Association
1740 Broadway
New York, NY 10019
(212) 315-8700
(800) LUNG-USA

American Parkinson's Disease Association (APDA)

Parkinson's disease is a debilitating nervous system disorder that affects close to three-quarters of a million people. APDA provides supportive programs for people with Parkinson's disease and works to find a cure for the disease. There are more than 80 chapters in the United States. Call their toll free number to find a program near you:

American Parkinson's Disease Association
1250 Hylan Blvd., Suite 4B
Staten Island, NY 10305
(718) 981-8001
(800) 223-2732

American Red Cross (ARC)

The American Red Cross is perhaps the finest example of the power of volunteerism. Through the organization, over 1.5 million volunteers provide invaluable services in a large number of areas related to health. Volunteers serve in over 2,700 chapters in and outside of the mainland United States, performing tasks such as administrative work, community health education, and helping in blood donor programs. Look in your local telephone book under American Red Cross to locate the chapter closest to you.

American Red Cross
National Headquarters
430 17th St. NW
Washington, DC 20006
(202) 737-8300

Amyotrophic Lateral Sclerosis (ALS) Association

The purpose of the ALS Association is to fight against the neurological condition that is often referred to as Lou Gehrig's disease, Amyotrophic Lateral Sclerosis. ALS is a progressive disorder that causes eventual paralysis and death. ALS has over 30 chapters nationwide. Call their toll free number to find the chapter close to you, or contact:

Amyotrophic Lateral Sclerosis Association
21021 Ventura Blvd., Suite 321
Woodland Hills, CA 91364
(818) 340-7500
(800) 782-4747

Arthritis Foundation (AF)

Arthritis has the dubious distinction of being the top chronic disease in the United States. The foundation's goals are to find cures for the numerous types of arthritis and to improve the lives of those who have it. To find the AF chapter in your area call the foundation's toll free number, or write to:

Arthritis Foundation
P.O. Box 19000
Atlanta, GA 30326
(800) 283-7800

Child Health Foundation (CHF)

CHF's goal is to improve the health of children through better medical care, and the prevention and treatment of disease. They particularly focus on areas of population that do not have adequate health care available.

Child Health Foundation
10630 Little Patuxent Parkway, Suite 325
Columbia, MD 21044
(301) 596-4514

Cystic Fibrosis Foundation

Cystic Fibrosis is an inherited disease that affects the pancreas, respiratory system, and apocrine glands. CF usually begins in infancy and often leads to an early death, although, for unknown reasons, males with the disease live longer than females. Volunteers work in more than 70 foundation chapters in the United States. For information call the foundation's toll free number, or look in your local telephone directory under Cystic Fibrosis Foundation.

Cystic Fibrosis Foundation
6931 Arlington Road
Bethesda, MD 20814
(301) 951-4422
(800) FIGHT-CF

Epilepsy Foundation of America (EFA)

EFA has a range of national and local programs to help people with epilepsy, a brain disorder characterized by sudden, brief losses of consciousness or motor activity, or sensory problems. Call their toll free number to find the chapter close to you:

Epilepsy Foundation of America
4351 Garden City Drive
Landover, MD 20785
(301) 459-3700
(800) EFA-1000

Huntington's Disease Society of America (HDSA)

Huntington's disease is an inherited disorder of the central nervous system that is characterized by increasing dementia. Its onset usually occurs at 30 to 50 years of age. Volunteers are welcome to help fight the disease at HDSA's chapters across the country. Call their toll free number to find out about volunteer opportunities near you or look in your local telephone book under Huntington's Disease Society of America.

Huntington's Disease Society of America
140 West 22nd St., 6th Floor
New York, NY 10011
(212) 242-1968
(800) 345-HDSA

Juvenile Diabetes Foundation International (JDF)

JDF works to prevent juvenile diabetes. There are more than 100 chapters in the United States. Call JDF's toll free number to find a program near you, or look in your local telephone book under Juvenile Diabetes Foundation.

Juvenile Diabetes Foundation International
120 Wall Street
New York, NY 10005
(212) 785-9500
(800) JDF-CURE

Lupus Foundation of America (LFA)

LFA has nearly 100 chapters across the United States organized to fight lupus, an autoimmune disease that affects primarily young women. Foundation chapters are run mostly by volunteers. Call the foundation's toll free number to find a program near you or look in your local telephone book under the Lupus Foundation of America.

Lupus Foundation of America
4 Research Place, Suite 180
Rockville, MD 20850
(301) 670-9292
(800) 955-4572

March of Dimes Birth Defects Foundation

The March of Dimes works to prevent birth defects and to reduce infant mortality. There are more than 130 March of Dimes chapters throughout the country. All chapters welcome volunteers. The March of Dimes toll free number is designated only for ordering multiple copies of supplies such as brochures.

March of Dimes Birth Defects Foundation
1275 Mamaroneck Ave.
White Plains, NY 10605
(914) 428-7100
(800) 367-6630
(to order multiple copies of supplies *only*)

National Kidney Foundation (NKF)

This association works to prevent diseases of the kidney and urinary tract. They have chapters throughout the United States. Call the foundation's toll free number to find a program near you or look in your local telephone book under the National Kidney Foundation.

National Kidney Foundation
30 East 33rd St.
New York, NY 10016
(212) 889-2210
(800) 622-9010

Sickle Cell Disease Association of America, Inc.

The Sickle Cell Disease Association works to inform the public about sickle cell anemia, a hereditary chronic blood disease. The disease affects Mediterranean, African, and African-American populations. It can interfere with the development of children. The association has chapters throughout the United States. Call their toll free number to find a program near you or look in your local telephone book under Sickle Cell Disease Association.

Sickle Cell Disease Association of America, Inc.
200 Corporate Pointe, Suite 495
Culver City, CA 90230-7633
(310) 216-6363
(800) 421-8453

Sudden Infant Death Syndrome (SIDS) Alliance

Sudden Infant Death Syndrome is the unexpected, sudden death of an infant. It is the most common cause of death of a child between two weeks and one year old. Anyone who has experienced or knows someone who has experienced the tragic loss of a child or grandchild through SIDS understands the value of this organization, which works to prevent the syndrome. The SIDS Alliance has affiliated organizations throughout the United States. Call their toll free number to find a program near you or look in your local telephone book under Sudden Infant Death Syndrome Alliance.

Sudden Infant Death Syndrome Alliance
1314 Bedford Ave., Suite 210
Baltimore, MD 21200
(410) 653-8226
(800) 221-7437

The United Parkinson Foundation (UPF)

UPF sponsors support groups throughout the United States and supports research on the disease. Contact their national office for more information or look in your local telephone directory for United Parkinson Foundation support groups.

The United Parkinson Foundation
833 West Washington Blvd.
Chicago, IL 60607
(312) 733-1893

21

VOLUNTEER TO STOP AIDS AND HELP THOSE WHO HAVE IT

AIDS (Acquired Immune Deficiency Syndrome), the disease caused by HIV (human immunodeficiency virus) infection, is characterized by a severely weakened immune system that cannot fight off infections and cancer. HIV is highly contagious, but accidental infection is rare. The virus is transmitted by exchange of body fluids (e.g., semen, blood, saliva) or by transfusion of infected blood. AIDS can be prevented through taking well-defined precautions, such as never having unprotected sex with someone who might be infected.

One of the best things that you can do to prevent AIDS is to make sure that you, your family, and friends are aware of the risk factors to prevent the disease. Here is a summary of the major risk factors:

- Sharing drug needles or syringes. This includes needles used when shooting drugs into veins, tattooing, ear piercing, and shooting steroids.
- Having unprotected sex (sex without a condom) with an infected person or someone who you do not know is infected.
- Having another sexually transmitted disease, such as syphilis, herpes, chlamydia, or gonorrhea, also appears to make someone more susceptible to HIV infection during sex with an infected partner.

The following people are also high risk for contracting HIV infection:

- Individuals who received transfusions of blood or any blood product before 1984.
- Women who have been artificially inseminated with sperm from high risk individuals.
- Children of women infected with AIDS.

The organizations listed below are representative of the large number of programs that help inform people about how to prevent AIDS, work toward cures, and provide important support to adults and children who are infected. Most of these outstanding organizations are run by devoted volunteers.

Thousands of mainstream organizations, such as Parent Teacher Associations (PTAs), March of Dimes, National Urban League, National Council of La Raza, the American Red Cross, and Boys' Clubs and Girls' Clubs, are working hard on the local level to stop the spread of AIDS. In addition, many local organizations such as the San Francisco AIDS Foundation or AIDS Project Los Angeles provide important services within their communities. To find out about such organizations, look for them by name in your local telephone book or call your local health department. One of the best resources for locating volunteer opportunities to prevent AIDS or help those who are infected is the National AIDS Hotline listed in this key.

American Foundation for AIDS Research (AmFar)
This private organization is dedicated to funding AIDS research and policy development. Volunteers are needed to help with fund-raising.

American Foundation for AIDS Research
5900 Wilshire Blvd., 23rd Floor
Los Angeles, CA 90036
(213) 857-5900

733 Third Ave., 12th Floor
New York, NY 10017
(212) 682-7440

Gay Men's Health Crisis (GMHC)

This organization was one of the first to provide help to people with AIDS. They provide a full range of services from education to making treatments available to those who need them.

Gay Men's Health Crisis
129 W. 20th St.
New York, NY 10011
Hotline: (212) 807-6655
(212) 337-3593
(212) 645-7470 (TDD)

National AIDS Hotline

Hotline information specialists can refer you to groups in your area that welcome volunteers. They also can direct you to local counseling and testing centers, and tell you where to get educational materials. It is open 24 hours a day, and trained operators answer questions and send information. Call any of the hotline numbers here to find out about volunteer opportunities.

For AIDS information in English: (800) 342-AIDS
For AIDS information in Spanish: (800) 344-SIDA
Deaf Access: (800) AIDS-TTY
The National STD Hotline: (800) 227-8922
For information about clinical trials on HIV:
(800) TRIALS-A

The Names Project Foundation (TNPF)

The foundation is known for its AIDS memorial quilt. The quilt grows every year, and has thousands and thousands of panels dedicated to AIDS victims. To view sections of the quilt or find out how to volunteer for the project contact:

NAMES Project Visitor Center
2362 Market St.
San Francisco, CA 94114
National Office phone number: (415) 882-5500

Pediatric AIDS Foundation

This organization addresses the special problems of children with AIDS. It also helps fund AIDS research.

Pediatric AIDS Foundation
1311 Colorado Ave.
Santa Monica, CA 90404
(310) 395-9051

22

HELP PEOPLE WHO HAVE CANCER OR OTHER LIFE-THREATENING ILLNESSES

The following resources provide volunteer opportunities to work to stamp out life-threatening illnesses or to provide support for those who must cope with them. It includes a special section of programs for children and their parents. For information about volunteering for hospice programs see Key 28.

American Cancer Society (ACS)

Cancer is the number two killer in the United States. It has become so pervasive that about one in three Americans today will get the disease. The American Cancer Society is the major not-for-profit association working to prevent and cure the numerous varieties of cancer. More than 2 million volunteers work in 3,000 local ACS units to fight the disease and to provide help to its victims. Volunteers receive training. Check your local telephone book for a program near you or contact:

American Cancer Society
1599 Clifton Road
Atlanta, GA 30329
(404) 320-3333
(800) ACS-2345

The Leukemia Society of America (LSA)

This organization is devoted to curing leukemia and related cancers. The organization has about 60 chapters across the country. To find the chapter closest to you call the LSA toll free number, or contact:

The Leukemia Society of America
600 Third Avenue
New York, NY 10016
(212) 573-8484
(800) 955-4572

National Coalition for Cancer Survivorship (NCCS)
NCCS members are cancer survivors and their loved ones. NCCS provides information for cancer survivors and will help community groups get started.

National Coalition for Cancer Survivorship
1010 Wayne St., 5th Floor
Silver Spring, MD 20910
(301) 650-8868

Y-Me National Organization for Breast Cancer Information and Support (Y-Me)
This breast cancer support program provides a number of important services, including hotline counseling by trained volunteers and help for presurgical patients. Y-Me has chapters throughout the United States. Call their toll free number to find out how to help or contact their national headquarters:

Y-Me
212 West Van Buren
Chicago, IL 60607
(312) 986-8338
(800) 221-2141 (9 A.M.–5 P.M. central time, weekdays)
24-Hour National Crisis Hotline (312) 986-8228

Programs for Children and Their Families

Candlelighters Childhood Cancer Foundation (CCCF)
This support organization for parents of children with cancer helps the young victims' families cope with the disease and its treatments. There are more than 400 Candlelighters support groups across the country, run entirely by volunteers. Call the Candlelighters toll free number to find out how to volunteer for the organization.

Candlelighters Childhood Cancer Foundation
7910 Woodmont Ave., Suite 460
Bethesda, MD 20814
(301) 657-8401
(800) 366-2223

The Children's Wish Foundation (CWF)
Volunteers help children who are terminally ill fulfill their wishes. Call their toll free number to find out how to help or contact their national headquarters.

The Children's Wish Foundation (CWF)
7840 Roswell Road, Suite 301
Atlanta, GA 30350-4867
(404) 393-WISH
(800) 323-WISH

The Make-a-Wish Foundation of America
This foundation has granted more than 20,000 wishes to children who are dying or have life-threatening diseases. There are over 70 Make-a-Wish chapters in the United States. Call their toll free number to find out how to help or contact their national headquarters:

The Make-a-Wish Foundation of America
100 West Clarendon St., Suite 2200
Phoenix, AZ 85013-3518
(800) 722-WISH

The Holiday Project

Through the Holiday Project, thousands of volunteers visit sick and disabled people living in institutions during the major holidays such as Christmas and Hanukkah. Volunteers are needed all year long to wrap presents, visit people in institutions, or perform other important tasks. The Holiday Project should be listed in your telephone directory or contact:

The Holiday Project
P.O. Box 6347
Lake Worth, FL 33466-6347
(407) 966-5702

Ronald McDonald House

Ronald McDonald Houses provide housing and emotional support to families of sick children who must leave home to be near a hospital while a sick child receives medical care. Volunteers can help in countless ways including aiding families, providing transportation, and fund-raising. There are more than 150 Ronald McDonald Houses in the United States. Check your local phone book for a program near you or contact:

Ronald McDonald House
1 Kroc Drive
Oak Brook, IL 60521
(708) 575-7418

The Starlight Foundation

This international organization fulfills wishes and provides entertainment for seriously ill children ages 4 through 18. Starlight has chapters in a number of cities in the United States, and in Australia, England, and Canada.

Starlight Foundation
12233 West Olympic Blvd., Suite 322
Los Angeles, CA 90064
(310) 207-5558

The Sunshine Foundation

The Sunshine Foundation includes 30 chapters that grant the wishes of seriously ill children ages 3 to 11. Call their toll free number to find out if there is a chapter near you or contact:

The Sunshine Foundation
2001 Bridge St.
Philadelphia, PA 19124
(215) 535-1413
(800) 767-1976

23

HELP THE BLIND AND HARD OF HEARING

Millions of Americans have problems with either their hearing or vision, or both. Estimates are that over 21 million people in the United States are deaf or hard of hearing and over 3 million have severe vision problems. Many people develop these conditions as they age.

This key covers three types of programs that need dedicated volunteers—those for the blind, the deaf, and the deaf/blind. All of these programs welcome volunteers, particularly those experienced in helping people with vision or hearing problems. If you are interested in helping people who are blind, also see Key 16, which covers information on the Guide Dog Foundation for the Blind and Guided Eyes for the Blind.

It is important to remember that there are many things you can do on your own to help the deaf or blind. For example, you could read to a blind neighbor, help blind or deaf friends with their shopping, or write letters to relatives and friends for nursing home residents who are visually impaired.

Programs for the Blind

American Council of the Blind (ACB)
ACB is an invaluable source of information for the blind and visually impaired, and those who wish to volunteer to help them. The Washington Connection, their toll free number, provides recorded updates on legislative and other issues that affect the blind and visually impaired.

ACB publishes a braille newsletter and provides other helpful publications. The ACB national office refers volunteers to local programs. If you call their toll free number between 3:30 and 5:00 P.M. Eastern Standard Time you can talk to a staff member directly.

American Council of the Blind
1155 15th St. NW, Suite 720
Washington, DC 20005
(202) 467-5081
(800) 424-8666

Association of Radio Reading Services

This organization includes about 135 radio reading services in the United States. The contact organization for the association will change periodically as new association presidents are elected, but if you call or write to the following they can tell you who to contact:

Association of Radio Reading Services
c/o 2100 Wharton St., Suite 140
Pittsburgh, PA 15203
(412) 488-3944

National Federation of the Blind (NFB)

NFB is the largest organization of the blind in the United States. Their goal is to integrate people who are blind or visually impaired into society. They publish a monthly magazine in braille, and have a catalog of braille and print publications. NFB also runs the Job Opportunities for the Blind (JOB) program in partnership with the U.S. Department of Labor. If you would like to hire a blind person, JOB is a great resource. Contact the national organization through their toll free number or the local chapter listed in your telephone directory to find out how to volunteer for other programs.

National Federation of the Blind
1800 Johnson St.
Baltimore, MD 21230
(410) 659-9314

National Industries for the Blind (NIB)

NIB is a corporation of over 100 associated industries helping blind and visually impaired people reach their potential. Volunteers can help with services offered by the industries such as job counseling, job training, and instruction in braille. Call NIB's toll free number to learn about industries in your area where you can volunteer:

National Industries for the Blind
1901 N. Beauregard St., Suite 200
Alexandria, VA 22311-1705
(703) 998-0770
(800) 433-2304

Prevent Blindness America (PBA)

Prevent Blindness is dedicated to ending blindness in the United States. It offers a number of important programs such as a toll free telephone number that provides information on eye health, vision screenings in local areas, and funding of research. Volunteers play an important role in the Prevent Blindness organization, particularly in affiliate programs throughout the country. Call PBA's toll free number to find an affiliate near you:

Prevent Blindness America
500 East Remington Road
Schaumburg, IL 60173
(847) 843-2020
(800) 331-2020

Recording for the Blind and Dyslexic Inc.

This organization serves thousands of people every year who cannot read due to a visual or related problem. With the help of this exemplary group, many print-disabled students have progressed through school and college to the graduate degree level. Among other tasks, volunteers read and record textbooks and other printed material, and maintain recording equipment. There are over 30 recording programs now operating, and RFB volunteers have recorded more than 4,000 books in these studios. Contact the Recording for the Blind and Dyslexic national headquarters to find out how to volunteer.

Recording for the Blind and Dyslexic Inc.
20 Roszel Road
Princeton, NJ 08540
(609) 452-0606

United States Association for Blind Athletes (USABA)

This association promotes athletic participation among the blind and visually impaired. There are close to 50 chapters in the United States. Through these chapters, blind athletes take part in a number of sports including swimming, track, and alpine skiing. Contact the headquarters in Colorado to find the program closest to you:

United States Association for Blind Athletes
  (USABA)
33 N. Institute St.
Colorado Springs, CO 80903
(719) 630-0422

Programs for the Deaf or Hard of Hearing

One useful way to help out someone who is deaf is to learn to train hearing dogs. There are a number of dog training programs throughout the United States, which are designed specifically to train dogs to aid the deaf.

Look in your local telephone book under canine training or dog training, or contact Paws With A Cause, listed next in this key.

Paws With A Cause

This wonderful organization trains service and hearing dogs in 32 regional offices throughout the United States. Call their toll free number to find a program near you:

Paws With A Cause
1235 100th St. SE
Byron Center, MI 49315
(616) 698-0688
(800) 253-PAWS

ADARA

ADARA formerly stood for the American Deafness and Rehabilitation Association. The organization is now called ADARA—Professionals Networking for Excellence in Service Delivery with Individuals Who Are Deaf or Hard of Hearing. The organization is a partnership of professionals, organizations, and others working to ensure that people who are deaf or hard of hearing receive the services they deserve. ADARA publishes a journal, newsletter, and directory of members. The directory is an excellent resource for volunteers.

ADARA
P.O. Box 251554
Little Rock, AR 72225-1554
(501) 868-8850

Alexander Graham Bell Association for the Deaf (AGBAD)

This organization works to encourage early detection of hearing loss in children, provides financial aid to deaf students, and works to promote legislation that is advantageous to the deaf. AGBAD provides publications with useful information for volunteers working with the deaf. Contact the national office to find out how you can contribute:

Alexander Graham Bell Association for the Deaf
3417 Volta Place NW
Washington, DC 20007
(202) 337-5220

National Association for the Deaf (NAD)

NAD is a large consumer organization for the deaf. They work to make sure that the deaf have the services they need and to influence legislation that affects the deaf. The association has 50 state affiliates that welcome volunteers. Look in your local telephone directory under your state's list of associations or contact the national office to find the program near you where you can volunteer.

National Association for the Deaf
814 Thayer Ave.
Silver Spring, MD 20910
(301) 587-1788

National Information Center on Deafness (NICD)

NICD is a clearinghouse for information on deafness, and it can guide you to programs in your area where you can volunteer.

National Information Center on Deafness
Gallaudet University
800 Florida Ave. NE
Washington, DC 20002
(202) 651-5051
(202) 651-5052 (TDD)

Deaf/Blind Programs

Helen Keller National Center for
Deaf-Blind Youths and Adults

The Helen Keller Center provides programs addressing the special needs for the deaf-blind. Their goal is to help people who are both deaf and blind to live full lives in their communities. The Center has ten regional offices and 30 affiliated agencies. Contact the national office to find a program near you where you can volunteer:

Helen Keller National Center for
  Deaf-Blind Youths and Adults
111 Middle Neck Road
Sands Point, NY 11050
(516) 944-8900

24

HELP PEOPLE WHO
ARE DISABLED

There are numerous volunteer opportunities in every community to help people who are or could become disabled, ranging from working to prevent certain causes of disability such as spina bifida, to providing direct assistance to people with handicaps, or organizing sports such as wheelchair tennis. The following organizations, serving children as well as adults, are representative of those found in communities across the country.

American Paralysis Association (APA)

APA's major purpose is to support research to cure paralysis. It provides a 24-hour hotline for people who are paralyzed by spinal cord injuries. The hotline refers callers to volunteers who have had similar experiences. APA has more than ten chapters in the United States. To find a program near you, check in your local telephone directory under Paralysis Association of (your state) or call APA's toll free number:

American Paralysis Association
500 Morris Ave.
Springfield, NJ 07081
(201) 379-2690
(800) 225-0292

The Association of Retarded Children (The ARC)

There are more than 7 million Americans with mental retardation. The Association of Retarded Children, commonly known as the ARC, is the largest organization that is dedicated to improving the welfare of these people. The ARC's goal is to help the mentally retarded reach their highest level of personal achievement. There are about 1,200 ARC chapters in the country where volunteers are always welcome. To find a program near you, check in your local telephone directory under The ARC or The Association of Retarded Children or contact:

The ARC
500 East Border St., Suite 300
Arlington, TX 76010
(817) 261-6003
(800) 433-5255

Brain Injury Association

This association works to prevent brain injuries and to help those who are brain injury survivors. They have programs in 46 states. To find an affiliate near you, check in your local telephone directory under Brain Injury Association of (your state) or call their toll free number:

Brain Injury Association
1776 Massachusetts Ave. NW, Suite 100
Washington, DC 20036
(202) 296-6443
(800) 444-6443

Family Friends

Family Friends, sponsored by the National Council on Aging (NCOA), has a number of volunteer programs for people age 55 and older. In one of their most innovative programs, volunteers are matched with children who are disabled or have a chronic illness. The volunteers visit the children once a week, spending four hours or more helping them take care of themselves, playing with them, helping them with their homework, or performing similar activities. Family Friends often become like grandparents to the families, and their activities with the children give their parents an important respite. Volunteers are reimbursed for transportation and extra meals at about $8 to $10 a visit.

Family Friends is a national program operating in 32 states. In addition to the program for disabled or chronically ill children, Family Friends also has projects in which volunteers work with the homeless, teenage mothers, and HIV-positive children.

If you do not have a Family Friends program in your area and you would like to start one, NCOA has a replication handbook called *Bring Family Friends to Your Community*. The handbook is free. To find a program in your area or to order a handbook, contact:

Family Friends
National Council on the Aging
409 Third St. SW
Washington, DC 20024
(202) 479-6675

Goodwill Industries International Inc.

Goodwill provides employment training and services for individuals with disabilities. Goodwill has programs throughout the United States, Canada, and in other countries where more than 14,000 volunteers donate their time. To find a program near you, check in your local telephone directory under Goodwill or call Goodwill's toll free number:

Goodwill Industries International
9200 Wisconsin Ave.
Bethesda, MD 20814
(301) 530-6500
(800) 741-0197

Multiple Sclerosis Association of America (MSAA)

Multiple Sclerosis (MS) is an inflammatory disease of the central nervous system. Symptoms can include weakness and numbness in the arms and legs, unsteady gait, vertigo, and vomiting. The association funds research, provides services and vocational training to individuals with MS, and many other services. Volunteers can provide direct help for people with multiple sclerosis or perform other services in the 50 chapters across the country. To find a chapter near you, check in your local telephone directory under Multiple Sclerosis or call MSAA's toll free number:

Multiple Sclerosis Association of America
706 Haddonfield Road
Cherry Hill, NJ 08002
(609) 488-4500
(800) 523-7667

The Muscular Dystrophy Association (MDA)

Through a variety of services including research, public education, and medical care, MDA fights 40 neuromuscular diseases that cause a wasting away and atrophy of muscles. MDA has affiliated clinical programs in hospitals throughout the United States, about 160 chapters, and about 80 summer camps. The Muscular Dystrophy Association is also known for the MDA Jerry Lewis Labor Day Telethon. To find a program near you check in your local telephone directory under Muscular Dystrophy Association or call MDA's toll free number:

The Muscular Dystrophy Association
3300 East Sunrise Drive
Tucson, AZ 85718
(520) 529-2000
(800) 572-1717

The National Easter Seal Society (NESS)

NESS is well known for its national network of programs that help people with disabilities to reach maximum independence. Services provided by the National Easter Seal Society include vocational training, education, social work, legislative lobbying, and advocacy. Volunteers provide valuable services in all aspects of Easter Seal programs. To find a program near you check in your local telephone directory under Easter Seals or call NESS's toll free number:

National Easter Seal Society
230 W. Monroe St., 18th Floor
Chicago, IL 60606
(312) 726-6200
(800) 221-6827

National Information Center for Children and Youth with Disabilities (NICHCY)

This organization uses the initials of its prior name, the National Information Center for Handicapped Children and Youth, as its acronym. NICHCY provides free information to those caring for children and youth with disabilities. They are a comprehensive resource on all disabilities such as Down's syndrome and spina bifida. Call its toll free number for information:

National Information Center for Children
 and Youth with Disabilities
P.O. Box 1492
Washington, DC 20013-1492
(202) 884-8200
(800) 695-0285

National Organization on DisAbility (NOD)

NOD works to improve attitudes toward individuals with disabilities. As a result of the organization's efforts, the governor in each state appoints an individual to forward the causes of people with disabilities. Look in your local telephone book for an affiliate near you or contact:

National Organization on DisAbility
910 16th St. NW, Suite 600
Washington, DC 20006
(202) 293-5960

Spina Bifida Association of America (SBAA)
Spina bifida is caused by the failure of the spinal bones to close during pregnancy. It is one of the most common birth defects leading to disability. SBAA has 72 chapters in the United States. To find a chapter near you check in your local telephone directory under Spina Bifida Association or call SBAA's toll free number:

Spina Bifida Association of America
4590 MacArthur Blvd. NW, Suite 250
Washington, DC 20007
(202) 944-3285
(800) 621-3141

The United Cerebral Palsy Association (UCPA)
Cerebral palsy is a movement and posture disorder caused by injury to the brain. UCP has over 150 state and local affiliates in the United States who work to better the lives of people with cerebral palsy. They also provide direct services to individuals who have cerebral palsy. To find a program near you, check in your local telephone directory under Cerebral Palsy Association of (your state) or call UCP's toll free number:

United Cerebral Palsy Association
1660 L St. NW, Suite 700
Washington, DC 20036-5602
(202) 776-0406
(800) 872-5827

Sports and Recreational Programs for the Disabled

The National Foundation of Wheelchair Tennis (NFWT)
This organization promotes the game of wheelchair tennis. Its programs include sports camps for disabled children. Contact the national office to find a program near you:

The National Foundation of Wheelchair Tennis
940 Calle St., Suite B
San Clemente, CA 92673
(714) 361-6811

Disabled Sports U.S.A.
This organization has chapters throughout the United States that provide year-round sports opportunities for people who are disabled. To find a program near you, check in your local telephone directory under Disabled Sports or call Disabled Sport's toll free number:

Disabled Sports U.S.A.
451 Hungerford Drive, Suite 100
Rockville, MD
(301) 217-0960
(800) 217-0960

The National Wheelchair Athletic Association (NWAA)
NWAA promotes a wide range of sports for people in wheelchairs. Contact the national office to find a program near you:

National Wheelchair Athletic Association
3595 East Fountain Blvd., Suite L-1
Colorado Springs, CO 80910
(719) 574-1150

The North American Riding for the Handicapped Association (NARHA)

NARHA is an organization of about 500 affiliated therapeutic riding centers that serve over 21,000 riders who are physically, mentally, or emotionally handicapped. NARHA centers are accredited, and trainers must receive certification to participate. To find a NARHA program near you check in your local telephone directory under Riding for the Handicapped or call their toll free number:

The North American Riding for
 the Handicapped Association
P.O. Box 33150
Denver, CO 80233
(303) 452-1212
(800) 369-7433

Shake-A-Leg (SAL)

Shake-A-Leg is an innovative sports and recreational organization for people who have spinal cord injuries and other forms of physical disability. The founder was paralyzed from an accident and formed the organization to improve the lives of people who are physically challenged. Emphasis is on body awareness and building confidence. SAL relies heavily on volunteers to put on its sports programs, which include sailing, horseback riding, swimming, and a variety of other sports. For information contact:

Shake-A-Leg
200 Harrison St.
Newport, RI 02840
(401) 849-8898

Special Olympics International (SOI)

This organization provides training and competition in a variety of sports for children and adults who are mentally retarded. SOI activities take place in and outside the

United States. Special Olympic programs are run by volunteers who are always needed. To find a program near you, check in your local telephone directory under Special Olympics or call SOI's toll free number:

Special Olympics International
1325 G St. NW, Suite 500
Washington, DC 20005
(202) 628-3630
(800) 700-8585

Whole Access

The goal of Whole Access is to increase the opportunity for outdoor recreation for people with disabilities. It is an international program that is a resource to park agencies and others on how to design accessibility for the handicapped. Outside the Redwood City, California area, Whole Access is particularly interested in finding volunteers who can work with them by computer.

Whole Access
517-A Lincoln Ave.
Redwood City, CA 94061
(415) 363-2647 (voice or TDD)

25

HELP STOP SUBSTANCE ABUSE

There are many volunteer programs throughout the United States that help people whose lives have been dramatically affected by substance abuse—whether it is their own, a loved one's, or a drunk driver's. Because of limited space, all of the many valuable organizations cannot be listed here. Examples include substance abuse groups for clergy, gay men, lesbian women, people with dual problems, such as substance abuse and a mental health problem, doctors, lawyers, and people who are Jewish, Catholic, Mexican-American, African-American, or Hispanic. Many areas also offer programs such as Potsmokers Anonymous and Pills Anonymous for people with a range of substance abuse problems. If these groups are available in your area they will be listed in your telephone directory. The following list is representative of the many excellent programs you can get involved in.

AA World Services (AA)

AA is the major organization for recovering alcoholics. Its premise is that alcoholics can solve their common problems through helping others and achieve sobriety through a 12-step program that includes sharing their experiences, strength, and hope. To find a program near you, look in your local telephone book under Alcoholics Anonymous.

AA World Services
475 Riverside Drive
New York, NY 10163
(212) 870-3400

Al-Anon Family Group Headquarters (AFG)

Al-Anon is the primary group for family and relatives of individuals with alcohol problems. It also operates Alateen for members age 12 to 20 whose lives have been adversely affected by someone else's drinking. Al-Anon programs are based on the 12-step program of Alcoholics Anonymous. To find a program near you, check in your local telephone directory under Al-Anon or call the AFG toll free number:

Al-Anon Family Group Headquarters
P.O. Box 862
Midtown Station
New York, NY 10018-0862
(212) 302-7240
(800) 356-9996

Alateen

See Al-Anon.

Alcohol and Drug Problems Association of North America (ADPA)

ADPA seeks to facilitate government and professional action in the fields of alcoholism, drug abuse, and related problems through exchange of information and promotion of legislation and standards.

Alcohol and Drug Problems Association
 of North America
1555 Wilson Blvd., Suite 300
Arlington, VA 22209
(703) 875-8684

American Council on Alcohol Problems (ACAP)

ACAP seeks long range solutions to the problem of alcoholism through education and legislation. It coordinates the work of 36 state affiliates. Contact the ACAP national office to locate the affiliate close to you:

American Council on Alcohol Problems
3426 Bridgeland Drive
Bridgeton, MO 63044
(314) 739-5944

Citizens for a Drug Free America (CDFA)

The goal of CDFA is to mobilize an effort to win the war on drugs and achieve a drug free America by the year 2000. Contact the national office to see how you can help:

Citizens for a Drug Free America
3595 Bayside Walk
San Diego, CA 92109-7451
(703) 207-9300

Cocaine Anonymous World Services (CAWS)

This multinational program is based on the same premise as Alcoholics Anonymous (see page 127). Cocaine Anonymous has 2,000 groups that meet across the country. To find a program near you, check in your local telephone directory under Cocaine Anonymous or call the CAWS toll free number:

Cocaine Anonymous World Services
3740 Overland Drive, Suite H
Los Angeles, CA 90034-6337
(313) 559-5833
(800) 347-8998

Just Say No International

Just Say No is an international organization of local clubs for children ages 5 to 18. Formerly the Just-Say-No Foundation, it includes ten regional groups in the United States that provide assistance for local groups. It also conducts important research in primary prevention of addictions such as tobacco, alcohol, and illegal substance abuse, dropouts, and teenage pregnancy. To find a program near you, check in your local telephone directory under Just Say No or call their toll free number:

Just Say No International
2101 Webster St., Suite 1300
Oakland, CA 94612
(510) 939-6666
(800) 258-2766

Mothers Against Drunk Driving (MADD)

MADD is a grassroots organization founded by an advocate whose daughter was killed by a drunk driver. MADD works to stop drunk driving and has had great success in publicizing the problem, although much more needs to be done. To find a program in your area, look in your local telephone directory under Mothers Against Drunk Driving or call MADD's toll free number:

Mothers Against Drunk Driving
511 East John Carpenter Freeway, Suite 700
Irving, TX 75062-8187
(214) 744-MADD
(800) Get-MADD

Narcotics Anonymous (NA)

NA has over 500,000 members who use the 12-step method of Alcoholics Anonymous to recover from their addiction to narcotics. To find a program near you, look in your local telephone directory under Narcotics Anonymous or contact the national office:

Narcotics Anonymous
P.O. Box 9999
Van Nuys, CA 91409
(818) 780-3951

National Association on
Drug Abuse Problems (NADAP)

Among other things, NADAP is a clearinghouse and referral bureau for individuals, corporations, and local communities interested in the prevention and treatment of substance abuse. The organization is sponsored by business and labor organizations. Contact NADAP's office in New York City to see how you can help:

National Association on Drug Abuse Problems
355 Lexington Ave.
New York, NY 10017
(212) 986-1170

National Council on Alcoholism and
Drug Dependence (NCADD)

Through the national office and 170 local groups, NCADD works for the prevention and control of alcoholism through education and advocacy. They have an extensive publication list including "What Are the Signs of Alcoholism?" and a monthly newsletter. To find a program near you, call their toll free number:

National Council on Alcoholism and
 Drug Dependence
12 West 21st St.
New York, NY 10010
(212) 206-6770
(800) NCA-CALL

Partnership for a Drug Free America (DFA)

DFA is a coalition of individuals and organizations representing the advertising, production, and communications industry. The organization seeks to change social attitudes toward illegal drugs through the creative skills of their members. Among other things, it runs media antidrug advertisements depicting an egg being fried as a comparison of what drugs do to the brain. Contact DFA's office in New York City to see how you can help:

Partnership for a Drug Free America
405 Lexington Ave.
New York, NY 10174
(212) 922-1560

Rational Recovery Systems (RRS)

RRS is an alternative approach to Alcoholics Anonymous for recovery from substance abuse and other addictive behavior. RRS has more than 1,000 local self-help groups that teach people how to become emotionally independent from alcohol, chemicals, or food. Its premise is that the individual has the power to overcome addiction, rather than relying on spiritualism. RRS uses a system called the addictive voice recognition technique (AVRT) to help people reject irrational thoughts and beliefs that impede recovery. To find a program near you, look in your local telephone directory under Rational Recovery or contact the national office:

Rational Recovery Systems
P.O. Box 800
Lotus, CA 95651
(916) 621-4374

Women for Sobriety (WFS)

WFS includes 450 self-help groups across the country for women alcoholics who use a program based on abstinence. The program recognizes the difference between men and women in coping with drinking problems. To find a program near you, call their toll free number:

Women for Sobriety
P.O. Box 618
Quakertown, PA 18951
(215) 536-8026
(800) 333-1606

26

HELP PEOPLE WHO HAVE MENTAL HEALTH PROBLEMS

Mental health problems are perhaps the most lonely and isolating of health problems. Depending upon your interests, if you would like to help people with depression, anxiety, schizophrenia, obsessive-compulsive disorder or related problems, look in your local telephone directory under mental health services or suicide prevention. It is likely that you will find a full range of community programs that could use your assistance. In addition, here is a list of national organizations, many of whom have local affiliates, that would welcome your volunteer participation. Suicide prevention programs appear at the end of this key. Information on how to volunteer to help people affected by substance abuse appears in Key 25.

Mental Health Problems

Alliance for the Mentally Ill
This organization of mentally ill persons and their families works to inform the public about mental illness and to enhance the lives of the mentally ill. Contact the Alliance's office in Virginia to find out how you can help:

Alliance for the Mentally Ill
200 N. Glebe Road, Suite 1001
Arlington, VA 22203-3754
(703) 524-7600

Compeer

This international program matches volunteers with people who are mentally ill for a one-to-one friendship. Volunteers make a commitment of at least one hour a week for a year or more. Volunteers receive training. There are about 100 Compeer programs throughout the United States. To find a program near you look in your local telephone directory under Compeer, or contact:

Compeer
259 Monroe St., Suite B-1
Rochester, NY 14607
(716) 546-8280

Depression and Related Affective Disorders Association (DRADA)

This association provides services for people with affective disorders, which include depressive illnesses and manic-depression. It also serves the families and friends of these individuals, and mental health professionals. Programs include referral services, education, and consultation. Call the DRADA office at Johns Hopkins University in Baltimore for information on how to help:

Depression and Related Affective
  Disorders Association
Johns Hopkins Hospital, Meyer 3-181
600 N. Wolfe St.
Baltimore, MD 21287-7381
(410) 955-4647

Mental Illness Association

This foundation informs the public about mental illness. Among other things, it publishes a directory that lists mental illnesses and provides information on how to contact related associations. To order a directory contact:

Mental Illness Association
420 Lexington Ave., No. 2104
New York, NY 10170-0002
(212) 629-0755

National Alliance for the Mentally Ill (NAMI)

This alliance of about 1,000 self-help and advocacy groups is concerned with the problems of the severe and chronically mentally ill. NAMI's goals are to provide emotional support and practical guidance to families and to inform the public about mental illness. Contact their main office to find a program near you:

National Alliance for the Mentally Ill
2101 Wilson Blvd., Suite 302
Arlington, VA 22201
(703) 524-7600

National Depressive and Manic
Depressive Association (NDMDA)

This association provides support to mental health patients and their families and friends. Local groups conduct confidential rap sessions and meetings for patients and sponsor patient forums and lectures by health professionals. NDMDA maintains a toll free hotline for people seeking information.

National Depressive and Manic
  Depressive Association
730 N. Franklin, Suite 501
Chicago, IL 60610
(312) 642-0049
(800) 82-NDMDA

National Mental Health Association (NMHA)

This consumer advocacy association is devoted to fighting mental illness and promoting mental health. Among

135

other things, NMHA advocates funding for research and conducts public education. There are about 450 NMHA groups across the country that work with volunteers in programs and activities, such as visiting hospitals and other institutions, that help those who are mentally ill. Call the association's toll free number to find out about volunteer activities in your area:

National Mental Health Association
1021 Prince St.
Alexandria, VA 22314-2971
(703) 684-7722
(800) 969-NMHA

Obsessive-Compulsive Foundation (OCF)

This organization for people with obsessive-compulsive disorder—a chronic condition characterized by uncontrollable recurrent unpleasant thoughts and/or repetitive behaviors—seeks to find a cure or to control the disorder. The organization has five state groups and about 8,000 members. Contact OCF's headquarters in Connecticut to find out how you can help:

Obsessive-Compulsive Foundation
P.O. Box 70
Milford, CT 06460-0070
(203) 878-5669

Suicide Prevention

American Association of Suicidology (AAS)

This organization works to understand and prevent suicide and life-threatening behavior. AAS has five regional groups, all of which are dedicated to preventing suicide. Heartbeat, an affiliated program, provides support for persons who have lost a loved one through suicide. Contact the AAS national office to find out how you can help:

American Association of Suicidology
2459 South Ash St.
Denver, CO 80222
(303) 692-0985

American Suicide Foundation (ASF)

This group of medical professionals, community leaders, and suicide survivors provides funding for research on suicide. It trains professionals on how to treat suicidal individuals and offers support programs for suicide survivors. Call their toll free number to find out how you can help:

American Suicide Foundation
1045 Park Ave.
New York, NY 10028-1030
(212) 410-1111
(800) 531-4477

Youth Suicide Prevention (YSP)

This volunteer network works to increase awareness of youth suicide. Among other things, YSP publicizes the warning signals of suicide and assists in the development of youth suicide prevention programs. Contact the national office to find a program near you:

Youth Suicide Prevention
11 Parkman Way
Needham, MA 02192-2863
(617) 738-0700

27

VOLUNTEER TO DONATE YOUR BLOOD, ORGANS, AND TISSUES

When you volunteer to donate your blood or, upon your death, your tissues and organs, you are indeed volunteering a gift of life, sight, hearing, or walking. The need for blood, tissue, and organ donations is increasing due to the burgeoning number of lifesaving techniques that the medical profession is developing every year. Volunteering to donate organs and tissues is as easy as signing your name on a donor card. Such cards can be obtained through the resources listed here.

American Red Cross Blood Centers
The American Red Cross has blood centers throughout the United States. To find a center near you look in your telephone directory under American Red Cross or contact:

American Red Cross
National Headquarters
430 17th St. NW
Washington, DC 20006
(202) 737-8300

American Red Cross National Tissue Services
Through Red Cross Centers throughout the United States, human tissues are donated to thousands of recipients. Call the American Red Cross National Tissue Services toll free number to find out how to donate and to obtain donor cards:

American Red Cross National Tissue Services
4050 Lindell Blvd.
St. Louis, MO 63108
(314) 289-1155
(800) 2-TISSUE

Center for Organ Recovery and Education (CORE)

CORE develops and executes educational and medical/surgical programs designed to increase organ donations. CORE teams are available around the clock for organ and tissue retrieval from hospitals in western Pennsylvania, West Virginia, eastern Ohio, and southern New York. CORE also supplies access to the national computer system for matching and distributing organs such as hearts and lungs. Call CORE's toll free number to find out how you can help:

Center for Organ Recovery and Education
204 Silema Drive
Pittsburgh, PA 15238
(800) 366-6777

Eye Bank Association of America (EBAA)

Each year more than 40,000 people receive the gift of sight through the EBAA. Contact their office in Washington, DC, to find out how you can volunteer to donate:

Eye Bank Association of America
1725 I St. NW, Suite 308
Washington, DC 20006
(202) 775-4999

LifeBanc

LifeBanc will provide you with the information you need to become a donor of tissues and organs. They also offer "Key to Life" key rings and donor cards. Call their toll free number to find out how you can volunteer to donate:

LifeBanc
1909 E. 101st St.
Cleveland, OH 44106
(216) 791-LIFE
(800) 558-LIFE

The Living Bank (TLB)

This organization maintains the largest computerized multi-organ and tissue donor registry in the world, operating in all 50 states and 63 foreign countries. TLB can also supply you with donor cards, medallions, key chains, and decals that will advise medical professionals that you are an organ donor. Call their toll free number, (800) 528-2971, to find out how you can volunteer to donate.

The National Kidney Foundation (NKF)

NKF will supply you with a donor card if you are interested in donating your kidneys upon your death. They are also an excellent source of information on kidney disease. Call their toll free number to find out how you can volunteer to donate your kidneys:

The National Kidney Foundation
30 East 33rd St.
New York, NY 10016
(212) 378-2044
(800) 622-9010

National Marrow Donor Program (NMDP)

NMDP operates a computerized database to match potential donors with individuals who need bone marrow transplants. Call their toll free number to find out how you can volunteer to donate:

National Marrow Donor Program
3433 Broadway St. NE
Minneapolis, MN 55413
(612) 378-2044
(800) 526-7809

28

VOLUNTEER IN A HOSPITAL OR HOSPICE

This key covers two volunteer options—working in a hospital or a hospice. If you undertake either option you will bring comfort to patients who are sick and in need of attention, companionship, and cheer. Nursing home volunteering is covered in Key 19.

Hospitals

There are many tasks that you could undertake as a hospital volunteer. Here is a list of ideas:

- Join a hospital auxiliary, which offers a variety of volunteer options.
- Serve on a board of a not-for-profit hospital.
- Help with fund-raising.
- Take your pet and visit patients. (However, get approval for this first through hospital administration.) You also might want to work through one of the organizations such as the Pets Partners Program or a similar organization in your area. Contact the Pets Partners Program through the Delta Society, 289 Perimeter Road East, Renton, WA 98055-1329, (206) 226-7357, (800) 869-6898.
- If you have any special talents in areas such as puppetry, miming, or arts and crafts, see if you can organize regular visits at a children's hospital where you can put your talents to use with sick children.
- Be a friendly visitor—sometimes just sitting with a sick patient quietly, or at other times, talking or reading to the patient.
- Write letters to loved ones for patients.

- Run errands for patients.
- Escort patients to hospital events or the chapel.
- Serve as an interpreter for people who do not speak English, or, if you know sign language, for the deaf.
- Visit on holidays. Help decorate common areas for holidays.
- Bake cookies or other treats for patients who do not have dietary restrictions.

It is likely that you know about the hospitals that welcome volunteers in your area. If not, look in your local telephone directory under hospitals. Most hospitals have volunteer coordinators whom you can speak to directly to learn about options.

Here are some national resources and model programs:

Floating Hospital (FH)

This innovative program in New York City provides health services to homeless children and their families, children in foster care, and teens who engage in high-risk behaviors. The programs occur within a four-deck ship, docked in the East River at Wall Street. FH also offers health education and nutrition.

Floating Hospital
Pier 11
Wall at South St.
New York, NY 10005
(212) 514-7440

Hospital Audiences Inc. (HAI)

This innovative program has served 8 million people since it was founded in New York City in 1969. Similar programs have been replicated in Colorado and Texas. The program provides disabled people and others confined to nursing homes, hospitals, and other institutions with access to the arts and other public events. HAI receives low-cost or free tickets donated by a variety of services and arranges for transportation and supervision during the events. Volunteers serve as hosts and hostesses. For information on how to volunteer in New York, or to learn how to replicate the program in your area contact:

Hospital Audiences Inc. (HAI)
220 West 42nd St., 13th Floor
New York, NY 10036
(212) 575-7677

Volunteer Trustees of Not-for-Profit Hospitals

This organization is the communication network for volunteer trustees in not-for-profit hospitals. Its members include representatives of 155 not-for-profit hospitals and their voluntary governing boards. Contact the national office for more information.

Volunteer Trustees of Not-for-Profit Hospitals
818 18th St. NW, Suite 900
Washington, DC 20006
(202) 659-0338

Hospices

Hospices provide care for people in the final stages of a terminal illness and their families. The concept behind hospice care is to enable the patient to live as fully as possible. Hospices focus on the entire family as the unit of care. Their services are given in the home whenever possible, but institutional hospice care is available when needed.

Many of the activities that volunteers offer to hospital patients are also welcome in hospices. In addition, patients in home-based hospices often welcome the following help:

- running errands
- helping in the home, preparing meals, cleaning, and providing other domestic help

- taking the patient to appointments or visiting when appropriate
- learning skills in bereavement counseling, or, if you already have these skills, providing help working through grief with the patient and family members

To locate a hospice in your area, look in your local telephone directory under hospices. Like hospitals, most hospices have volunteer coordinators whom you can speak to directly to learn about options.

Hospice Association of America (HAA)

HAA promotes the concept of hospice, as described at the beginning of this section. HAA's members include hospices, home health agencies, community cancer centers, and health professionals with an interest in hospice care. The association provides forums on how to start up hospice programs. HAA is affiliated with the National Association for Home Care. Contact HAA's national office for more information:

Hospice Association of America
519 C St. NE
Washington, DC 20002
(202) 546-4759

National Hospice Organization (NHO)

The National Hospice Organization's membership consists of most of the hospices in the United States. Call NHO's toll free hotline to find a hospice in your area:

National Hospice Organization
1901 N. Moore St., Suite 901
Arlington, VA 22209
(703) 243-5900
(800) 658-8898

29

VOLUNTEER TO HELP VICTIMS OF CRIME

In addition to the physical injury and loss of goods that results from an assault, crime victims and witnesses often suffer tremendous emotional stress and can take a long time to recover from this. There are many supportive services that you can provide for individuals who are trying to cope with these problems. For example, you could:

- Volunteer in a rape crisis center, battered women's shelter, center for abused children, or other center that helps victims.
- Volunteer to help an individual or family who is recovering from the effects of a crime. For example, you could babysit while family members attend a counseling session, or accompany victims to court or the doctor's office, or help in other ways.
- Work on a hotline for crime victims.
- Learn about the special problems of crime victims so that you can provide what is needed at the appropriate time. A number of the resources listed below provide materials and programs that can help you learn skills to help crime victims.

Institute for Victims of Crime (IVC)

This group of professionals specializes in post-traumatic stress, crisis intervention, and the study of terrorism. IVC is a nonpolitical group that assists victims of terrorism, accidents, and natural and man-made disasters, as well as victims' families, friends, and associates. IVC is "committed to respond forcefully, effectively, and quickly to the increasing incidence of stress disorders resulting from the experiences of victims." The institute provides training in crisis intervention, emergency services, diagnosis and treatment, and counseling for professionals and paraprofessionals. Contact IVC's office in McLean, Virginia, for more information:

Institute for Victims of Crime
6801 Market Square Drive
McLean, VA 22101
(703) 847-8456

National Association for
Crime Victims' Rights (NACVR)

NACVR is an association of local businesses, professional groups, and others that seeks to "reverse the over-concern for criminals' rights at the expense of victims' rights." Among other things, it holds victimization seminars and self-defense training programs. The association includes nine state groups. Contact NACVR's office in Portland, Oregon, for more information:

National Association for Crime Victims' Rights
P.O. Box 16161
Portland, OR 97216-0161
(503) 252-9012

National Coalition Against Sexual Assault (NCASA)

NCASA is working to build a network of individuals and organizations concerned with sexual assault. The coalition acts as an advocate for and on behalf of rape victims and sponsors Sexual Assault Awareness Month in April. NCASA presently has six regional groups. Contact their office in Harrisburg, Pennsylvania, to find a program near you:

National Coalition Against Sexual Assault
912 N. Second St.
Harrisburg, PA 17102
(717) 232-6745

National Institute of Victimology (NIV)

NIV provides information and assistance to victims, witnesses, volunteers, and others concerned about crime and its effects. The institute works to improve victim and witness services. It publishes the quarterly journal *Victimology: An International Journal* and provides information on the dynamics of victimization. Contact NIV's headquarters to see how you can help:

National Institute of Victimology
2333 N. Vernon St.
Arlington, VA 22207
(703) 528-3387

National Organization for Victim Assistance (NOVA)

NOVA is an umbrella organization for groups interested in crime issues. Its stated purpose is to "express forcefully the victims' claims, too long ignored, for decency, compassion, and justice; to press those claims for the victims of crime and also for the victims of other stark misfortunes; and to ensure that victims' rights are honored by government officials and all others who can aid in the victims' relief and recovery."

NOVA provides direct assistance to victims and offers technical counsel, referral services, and victim assistance training programs. The organization sponsors the Regional Victim Assistance Training Program and National Victim Rights Week. NOVA also publishes a comprehensive list of victim services, *The Directory of Victim Assistance Programs.* Call NOVA's toll free number to find out how you can volunteer in your area:

National Organization for Victim Assistance
1757 Park Road NW
Washington, DC 20010
(202) 232-6682
(800) TRY-NOVA

National Victim Center (NVC)

NVC is a national resource center that seeks redress for crime victims. The center promotes victims' rights and victim assistance, public awareness, judicial responsiveness, and social service referrals for crime victims. NVC offers national referrals for crime victims to attorneys and has a comprehensive database of local organizations that can provide assistance to victims. It also is a great resource for the development of community-based programs for victims of crime. Contact NVC's office in Arlington, Virginia for information:

National Victim Center
2111 Wilson Blvd., Suite 300
Arlington, VA 22201
(703) 276-2880

Salvation Army

This organization focuses on a love of God and helping people in need. It includes more than 10,000 centers in the United States, which, among other things, provide emergency shelter for victims of crime. Look in your local telephone directory under Salvation Army to find a program near you, or contact:

The Salvation Army
National Headquarters
615 Slaters Lane
P.O. Box 269
Alexandria, VA 22313
(703) 684-5500

Women Against Rape (WAR)

WAR works toward the prevention of rape, and sponsors crisis intervention services and rape survivor support groups. Contact their office in Columbus, Ohio, to find out how to start a program in your area:

Women Against Rape
Box 02084
Columbus, OH 43202
(614) 291-9751

30

VOLUNTEER FOR DISASTER RELIEF

Whatever the cause, when disaster strikes, there is always a great need for volunteer assistance. There are many ways you can help. Immediately after an earthquake, hurricane, or other natural disaster, you can help organize food and necessities drives, find housing for displaced victims, or help in hospitals or other health institutions. You can also help *before* disasters occur by assisting agencies such as the Red Cross with fund-raising and other administrative needs, so that the resources they need are available to them when they need them. The following organizations are dedicated to helping the victims of disasters in and outside the United States.

American Radio Relay League Inc. (ARRL)

This league is a worldwide volunteer group of about 180,000 amateur radio operators. They provide help with communications during disasters when other lines of communication are not working. For information on how to volunteer as a radio operator contact:

American Radio Relay League Inc.
225 Main St.
Newington, CT 06111
(203) 666-1541

American Red Cross

The American Red Cross is known as the premier volunteer emergency services organization. In operation for more than 130 years, it has 2,600 chapters in the United

States. Volunteers are welcome to perform a wide variety of services including assisting in blood centers, teaching first aid, and helping repair homes that are damaged by natural causes. They also help people contact loved ones in or outside of the United States if disaster strikes. Training is provided for volunteers.

American Red Cross
National Headquarters
430 17th St. NW
Washington, DC 20006
(202) 737-8300

AmeriCares Foundation (AF)

AmeriCares is a relief organization dedicated to saving lives and fulfilling emergency medical needs worldwide. Since 1982 the organization has sent $1 billion in medical and pharmaceutical aid to disaster areas. Volunteers deliver the supplies to clinics, hospitals, and orphanages around the world. Call the AmeriCares toll free number to find out how to volunteer:

AmeriCares Foundation
161 Cherry St.
New Canaan, CT 06840
(203) 966-5195
(800) 486-HELP

CARE

Originally founded to send aid to World War II victims in Europe, this international aid and development organization provides food, disaster aid, and health care overseas. CARE maintains volunteer committees in several U.S. cities and 12 regional and district offices, and it operates in 39 developing countries in Asia, Africa, and Latin America. Call the CARE toll free number to find out how to volunteer, or contact:

151

CARE
151 Ellis St.
Atlanta, GA 30303
(404) 681-2552
(800) CARE-85

Feed the Children (FTC)

FTC is an international hunger and disaster relief organization with 17 offices throughout the world. The organization provides food, clothing, educational materials, medical equipment, and other necessities in the United States and 67 other countries to people struck by disasters such as floods, famine, or war. Call Feed the Children's toll free number to find out how to volunteer:

Feed the Children
Box 36
Oklahoma City, OK 73101-0036
(405) 942-0228
(800) 627-4556

Friends Disaster Service (FDS)

This volunteer group provides volunteer cleanup and restoration services to communities devastated by natural disasters. FDS efforts give priority to the elderly, disabled, low-income, and uninsured disaster victims.

Friends Disaster Service
241 Keenan Rd.
Peninsula, OH 44264
(216) 650-4975

Mountain Rescue Association (MRA)

If you live in a mountainous area, particularly one that attracts a lot of recreational climbers, you probably are well aware of the importance of this organization's operations. MRA has units throughout the United States and

Canada that perform mountain rescues. The association is also the central coordination agency for such rescues. Each unit has 25 members, at least five of whom have had experience with rescues over 10,000 feet, and are trained in approved techniques. Contact MRA's office in Salt Lake City, Utah to find out how you can volunteer:

Mountain Rescue Association
2144 South 1100 East, Suite 150-375
Salt Lake City, UT 84106
(303) 567-0450

National Fire Protection Association (NFPA)
This association of 65,000 members includes fire fighters, business and industry representatives, health care professionals, architects, and others interested in fire prevention. It develops and publishes standards to minimize the effects of fire and explosion. NFPA also conducts fire prevention and safety programs for the general public and sponsors National Fire Prevention Week each October. For information on how you can help promote fire safety contact:

National Fire Protection Association
1 Batterymarch Park
P.O. Box 9101
Quincy, MA 02269-9101
(617) 770-3000

National Safety Council (NSC)
NSC promotes accident reduction and disaster prevention by the exchange of information on safety and health. It offers a large number of publications on a wide range of disaster prevention and safety issues, including newsletters and prevention manuals for various industries.

National Safety Council
112 Spring Lake Drive
Itasca, IL 60143-3201
(708) 285-1121

Need Inc.

This international organization provides disaster relief, food distribution, and medical and building supplies primarily in Southeast Asia. NEED supports a school and health clinic in Calcutta, India. Contact NEED's office in Phoenix, Arizona to find out how you can help:

Need Inc.
12601 N. Cave Creek Rd.
P.O. Box 54541
Phoenix, Arizona 85078
(602) 992-1321

Presiding Bishop's Fund for World Relief (PBF/WR)

This arm of the Episcopal Church responds to natural disasters and other emergencies and communicates appeals for help during times of need. Through rehabilitation grants, the fund provides backup relief following crises. Check with your local Episcopalian church or call the fund's toll free number to find out how to volunteer:

Presiding Bishop's Fund for World Relief
815 Second Ave.
New York, NY 10017
(212) 992-5129
(800) 334-7626

U.S.A. for Africa (USAFA)

USAFA is an organization of American rock, pop, and country recording artists who work to raise money for victims of famine in Africa. The organization is known for organizing the song "We Are the World," written by

Michael Jackson and Lionel Richie. The group raises money through the sale of "We Are the World" recordings, shirts, posters, and videocassettes, and through donations. Contact USAFA's office in Los Angeles to find out how you can help:

U.S.A. for Africa
5670 Wilshire Blvd., Building 1450
Los Angeles, CA 90036-5614
(213) 954-3123

31

VOLUNTEER TO HELP IMMIGRANTS AND REFUGEES

There are many organizations to choose from if you want to help refugees and immigrants in or outside of the United States. Some of the tasks you can assist with are locating housing, interpreting, tutoring, helping to find education, and gaining access to needed services such as medical care. The following list is representative of many agencies throughout the world. Also check with local churches, synagogues, or other religious organizations. They often actively participate in programs for refugees and immigrants.

American Refugee Committee (ARC)
ARC's goal is to ensure the survival, health, and well-being of refugees, displaced persons, and others affected by mass population movements. ARC works with host countries to provide basic medical care and health care training. Contact ARC's office in Minneapolis to find out how you can help:

American Refugee Committee
2344 Nicollett Ave. S., Suite 350
Minneapolis, MN 55404
(612) 872-7060

Catholic Relief Services
U.S. Catholic Conference (CRS-USCC)
Catholic Relief Services is an official overseas organization of the American Catholic community. Among other

things, it conducts disaster response and refugee relief and rehabilitation. Active in 67 countries, CRS distributes food, clothing, and medicine. USCC has about 40 agencies in the United States. Ask your local parish how to get in touch with the agency near you or contact:

Catholic Relief Services
209 West Fayette St.
Baltimore, MD 21201
(410) 625-2220

Church World Service (CWS)

Church World Service has about 50 refugee service programs run by Protestant Christian churches. Check with the CWS headquarters in New York to find a program near you:

Church World Service
475 Riverside Drive
New York, NY 10115
(212) 870-2061

International Rescue Committee (IRC)

IRC dates back to 1933 and Hitler's regime in Germany, when Albert Einstein sought a way to help people fighting against the Nazis. Today IRC helps refugees throughout the world. The organization relies on volunteers in refugee camps and other programs throughout the world and in its resettlement offices in the United States. IRC particularly needs volunteers with backgrounds in health or teaching and with experience in setting up refugee camps. Contact IRC at their New York headquarters to find out how you can help:

International Rescue Committee
122 East 42nd St.
New York, NY 10168
(212) 551-3000
(212) 867-2837

Lutheran Immigration and Refugee Service (LIRS)

LIRS is an advocate for immigrants and refugees. It locates foster homes for refugees who are minors and offers counseling on immigration. The service has 26 regional groups in the United States. Ask your local Lutheran church how to get in touch with the agency near you or contact:

Lutheran Immigration and Refugee Service
390 Park Ave. South
New York, NY 10016-8803
(212) 532-6350

Refugees International (RI)

RI provides advocacy, information, education, and community support to refugees and others around the world. The organization operates emergency needs assessment programs and assists other refugee relief and assistance programs. RI promotes voluntary help through donation of funds, sponsorship of refugee families, medical services, and other programs. Call Refugees International's toll free number to find out how you can help or contact:

Refugees International
21 Dupont Circle NW
Washington, DC 20036
(202) 828-0110
(800) REF-UGEE

Refugee Voices (RV)

Refugee Voices is a campaign to educate Americans about the plight of refugees. It emphasizes the contributions to society that refugees make and acts as a clearinghouse for groups aiding refugees. In order to document the difficulties of refugees, RV produces a radio program and videotapes featuring interviews with refugees. Call the organization's toll free number to find out how you can help:

158

Refugee Voices
3041 Fourth St. NE
Washington, DC 20017-1102
(202) 832-0020
(800) 688-7338

Other Programs to Consider
Contact these organizations if you are interested in a
more specialized refugee or immigration program:

Afghanistan Refugee Committee (ARC), 667 Madison
Ave., 18th Floor, New York, NY 10021, (212) 355-2931

Aid for Afghan Refugees (AFAR), 32 West Minges
Road, Battle Creek, MI 49017, (616) 969-0754

American Medical Division, American Near East
Refugee Aid, 1522 K St. NW, Suite 202, Washington,
DC 20005, (202) 347-2558

American Fund for Czechoslovak Refugees (AFCR),
1776 Broadway, Suite 2105, New York, NY 10019,
(212) 265-1919

American Jewish Philanthropic Aid (AJFP), 122 East
42nd St., 12th Floor, New York, NY 10168-5640

American Near East Refugee Aid (ANERA), 1522 K St.
NW, Suite 202, Washington, DC 20005, (202) 347-2558

Association of Cambodian Survivors of America
(ACSA), 6616 Kerns Road, Falls Church, VA 22042,
(703) 532-7931

El Rescate, 1340 South Bonnie Brae, Los Angeles, CA
90006, (213) 387-3284

Ethiopian Community Development Council (ECDC),
1036 South Highland St., Arlington, VA 22204, (703)
685-0510

Guatemala Partners, 945 G St. NW, Washington, DC
20001, (202) 783-1123

Jesuit Refugee Service/U.S.A., 1424 16th St. NW, Suite
300, Washington, DC 20036, (202) 462-5200

Pontifical Mission for Palestine (PMP), 1011 First Ave., New York, NY 10022-4195, (212) 826-1480

Rav Tov International Jewish Rescue Organization (RTIJRO), 500 Bedford Ave., Brooklyn, NY 11211, (718) 963-1991

Southeast Asia Resource Action Center (SEARAC), 1628 16th St. NW, 3rd Floor, Washington, DC 20009, (202) 667-4690

Spanish Refugee Aid (SRA), 122 East 42nd St., 12th Floor, New York, NY 10168-1289, (212) 679-0010

Tibetan Aid Project (TAP), 2425 Hillside Ave., Berkeley, CA 94704, (510) 848-4238, (800) 33TIBET

U.S. Catholic Conference Migration and Refugee Services, 3211 Fourth St. NE, Washington, DC 20017-1194, (202) 541-3315

Vietnam Refugee Fund (VRF), 6433 Nothana Drive, Springfield, VA 22150, (703) 971-9178

32

VOLUNTEER TO SHARE YOUR PROFESSIONAL EXPERTISE

If you have corporate, small business, social service, or other professional experience you have a lot to offer organizations and businesses that could benefit from your expertise. For example, if your background is in social service, your present income is low, and you would like to get a small stipend for working in your community, the Senior Community Service Employment Program (SCSEP) could be a great way for you to contribute. Funded by the federal government, many organizations such as AARP and the National Council on Aging offer SCSEP programs around the country. Or, if you have corporate experience, you might want to look into the National Executive Service Clubs, which matches retirees with corporate and/or professional experience with nonprofit organizations in need of assistance in management and other areas.

The following list covers a number of important resources for professionals who would like to volunteer their expertise. Also check those keys that cover your particular area of expertise such as legal work (Key 9), the arts (Key 13), or education (Key 12).

Accountants for the Public Interest (API)

API encourages accountants to volunteer to help nonprofit groups and others who would have difficulty paying for their services. There are about 20 affiliates in the United States. To find out how you can help, contact the API headquarters in Washington, DC:

Accountants for the Public Interest
1012 14th St. NW, Suite 906
Washington, DC 20005
(202) 347-1668

Elder Craftsmen Inc.

This unique organization promotes fine handicrafts made by older people through Elder Craftsmen shops and cooperatives around the country that sell them.

Elder Craftsmen Inc.
135 East 65th St.
New York, NY 10021
(212) 861-5260

International Executive Service Corps (IESC)

The IESC sends retired U.S. executives and technical advisers all over the world to help developing nations build modern businesses. For information contact:

International Executive Service Corps
8 Stamford Forum
Stamford, CT 06904
(203) 967-6000

National Executive Service Corps (NESC)

NESC places retirees with corporate and/or professional experience to assist in nonprofit organizations, such as schools, arts organizations, and social service agencies. NESC has affiliates in over 20 states and Washington, DC.

National Executive Service Corps
257 Park Ave. South
New York, NY 10010
(212) 529-6660

Service Corps of Retired Executives (SCORE)

SCORE is sponsored by the Small Business Administration. It includes 760 offices and 13,000 volunteers nationwide that match retired executive volunteers with new entrepreneurs. Older veterans are an important client group. The organization provides information dissemination and professional education and training.

Service Corps of Retired Executives
409 Third St. SW, 4th Floor
Washington, DC 20024
(202) 205-6762 (or 7636)

Senior Community Service Employment Programs (SCSEP)

The SCSEP provides a small salary for community service to older people who meet low-income requirements. The following organizations sponsor SCSEP programs:

Senior Community Service Employment Program Sponsors:

American Association of Retired Persons
601 E St. NW
Washington, DC 20049
(202) 434-2277
FAX (202) 434-6470

Asociacion Nacional Pro Personas Mayores
3325 Wilshire Blvd., Suite 800
Los Angeles, CA 90010
LA office: (213) 487-1922
DC office: (202) 293-9329

Green Thumb Inc.
2000 N. 14th St., Suite 800
Arlington, VA 22201
(703) 522-7272

The National Caucus and Center on Black Aged Inc.
1424 K St. NW, Suite 500
Washington, DC 20005
(202) 637-8400

National Council of Senior Citizens
1331 F St. NW
Washington, DC 20004
(202) 624-9508

National Council on the Aging Inc.
409 Third St. SW, 2nd Floor
Washington, DC 20024
(202) 479-6631

National Indian Council on Aging Inc.
6400 Uptown Blvd. NE
City Centre, Suite 510 West
Albuquerque, NM 87110
(505) 242-9505

National Asian Pacific Center on Aging
Melbourne Tower, Suite 914
1511 Third Ave.
Seattle, WA 98101
(206) 624-1221

National Urban League
500 East 62nd St.
New York, NY 10021
(212) 310-9201 (or 9202)

U.S. Forest Service
1621 N. Kent St., Room 1010 RPE
Arlington, VA 22209
(703) 235-8855

33

VOLUNTEER FOR VOTERS' RIGHTS AND POLITICAL ACTION

Regardless of whether your politics lean to the right or the left, your volunteer action will be welcome by your political party, political action organizations such as Common Cause, or voters' rights projects such as Project Vote! This key lists examples of the types of organizations where you can volunteer and also exercise your political beliefs. If you are a Democrat, Republican, or belong to another political party, contact your state's party office to find out how you can volunteer. In addition, look into the American Civil Liberties Union, covered in Key 9.

AIDS Action Council (AAC)

AAC advocates in Washington, DC for more effective AIDS policy, legislation, and funding. The council represents more than 1,000 community-based AIDS organizations. Contact the AAC office in Washington, DC to find out how you can help:

AIDS Action Council
1875 Connecticut Ave. NW, Suite 700
Washington, DC 20009
(202) 986-1300

Americans for the Environment (AFE)

AFE is an educational organization that works to influence the formation of environmental policy through elections. The organization provides political and electoral skills training for environmental and conservation activists. Contact the AFE office in Washington, DC to find out how you can help:

Americans for the Environment
1400 16th St. NW
Washington, DC 20036
(202) 797-6665

Citizen Action Fund (CAF)

Formerly Citizen Action, CAF has a membership of 3 million people who work for economic democracy and social justice. The fund seeks more jobs, safe and affordable energy, fair taxes, equal voting rights, safe and healthy communities and toxic-free workplaces. CAF has 32 state groups. For information on how you can volunteer, look in your local telephone directory under Citizen Action Fund or contact their headquarters in Washington, DC:

Citizen Action Fund
1730 Rhode Island Ave. NW, Suite 403
Washington, DC 20036
(202) 775-1580

Common Cause (CC)

Common Cause is a citizens' lobby with 48 state groups and 250,000 members who work to improve government performance. Among other things, CC supports partial public financing of congressional election campaigns, nuclear arms control, and tax reform. CC lobbies to prevent the influence of political action committees (PACs) in Congress. For information on how you can volunteer for CC, look in your local telephone directory under Common Cause or contact the headquarters in Washington, DC:

Common Cause
2020 M St. NW
Washington, DC 20036
(202) 833-1200

Emily's List (EL)

The Emily in Emily's List stands for "early money is the yeast." EL is a political network that works to raise funds to support the election of Democratic women to political office. For information on how you can volunteer for EL, contact their headquarters in Washington, DC:

Emily's List
805 15th St., Suite 400
Washington, DC 20005-2207
(202) 326-1400

League of Women Voters (LWV)

The League of Women Voters is a nonpartisan organization dedicated to the full participation of citizens in government. LWV emphasizes voters' rights and providing forums for discussion of political issues. The League is active in all 50 states and most local areas on such issues as privacy in reproductive rights, voter registration, and sponsoring debates for candidates running for public office. Look in your local telephone directory under League of Women Voters, or contact LWV headquarters in Washington, DC, to find out how you can help:

League of Women Voters
1730 M St. NW
Washington, DC 20036
(202) 429-1965

Private Citizen Inc. (PCI)

This for-profit organization works to preserve the privacy of individuals through attempting to regulate junk phone calls and junk mail. PCI subscribers authorize the organization to notify telemarketers not to solicit them. If telemarketers persist in soliciting them, they are levied with a charge for their time. PCI also conducts lobbying for the regulation of telemarketing. Contact them at:

Private Citizen Inc. (PCI)
P.O. Box 233
Naperville, IL 60566
(708) 393-1555

Project Vote!

Project Vote! is a nonpartisan organization whose goal is to increase voting registration for low-income, minority, and unemployed citizens. The organization's activities include registering individuals door to door and in food stamp and unemployment lines. For information on how you can volunteer for Project Vote!, contact their headquarters in Washington, DC:

Project Vote!
1511 K St. NW, Suite 326
Washington, DC 20005
(202) 638-9016

United States Privacy Council (USPC)

USPC is an organization of individuals and groups committed to strengthening the right of privacy in the United States. It works to protect private records such as medical, insurance, and employment files. Contact USPC's Washington, DC office to find out how you can help:

United States Privacy Council
P.O. Box 15060
Washington, DC 20003
(202) 829-3660

34

VOLUNTEER FOR CIVIL RIGHTS

When you work on civil rights issues, you are helping to foster pride in the ethnic background of minorities. There are a great number of organizations working on civil rights issues. The following list is an overview of the types of groups that are available to volunteer with.

American Indian Heritage Foundation (AIHF)

AIHF works to aid American Indians through providing emergency relief and economic development. Among other things, the organization develops markets for American Indian handicrafts, helps to educate American Indian youth about their culture, and matches corporations with surpluses with Indian tribes in need through its Gifts-in-Kind Program. Contact the foundation's office in Virginia to find out how you can help:

American Indian Heritage Foundation
6051 Arlington Blvd.
Falls Church, VA 22044
(202) INDIANS

American Spanish Committee (ASC)

ASC is a group for Spanish-surnamed citizens. Among other things, it monitors the activities of international human rights groups and works to protect the rights of Spanish-surnamed Americans in the United States and abroad. Contact ASC through:

American Spanish Committee
P.O. Box 119
Canal Street Station
New York, NY 10013
(212) 567-7417

Anti-Defamation League (ADL)

ADL is a multinational group dedicated to stopping the defamation of Jewish people and to secure justice and fair treatment to all citizens. Among other things, it works to promote better interfaith and intergroup relations, works against anti-Semitism, and to strengthen democratic values and structures. The ADL has 28 regional groups. For information on volunteering, look in your local telephone directory under Anti-Defamation League, or contact their headquarters in New York:

Anti-Defamation League
823 United Nations Plaza
New York, NY 10017
(212) 490-2525

Center for Democratic Renewal (CDR)

CDR works for federal prosecution of the Ku Klux Klan. It seeks to build public opposition to racist groups and their activities. It works closely with other groups such as trade unions and religious groups. Contact them at:

Center for Democratic Renewal
P.O. Box 50469
Atlanta, GA 30302
(404) 221-0025

Center for Third World Organizing (CTWO)

CTWO helps low-income minority groups, such as Native-Americans and immigrants. Contact them at:

Center for Third World Organizing
1218 East 21st St.
Oakland, CA 94606-3132
(510) 533-7583

Chinese for Affirmative Action (CAA)

CAA is an organization of individuals and corporations seeking equal opportunity for and the protection of the civil rights of Asian-Americans. Among other things, the organization has worked in conjunction with state and local governments to develop bilingual materials to aid Asian-American job applicants. Contact CAA at:

Chinese for Affirmative Action
12 Walter U. Lum Place
San Francisco, CA 94108
(415) 274-6750

Commission for Social Justice (CSJ)

CSJ is the anti-defamation arm of the Order of Sons of Italy in America. It seeks to gain positive recognition for the contributions of Italians and Americans of Italian descent. CSJ has 35 state groups. Look in your telephone directory under Commission for Social Justice to find a program near you or contact:

Commission for Social Justice
219 E St. NE
Washington, DC 20002
(202) 547-2900

Klanwatch

Klanwatch's purpose is to gather and disseminate information about the Ku Klux Klan and to create a body of law to protect the rights of those the Klan is attacking. It collects information from 13,000 U.S. publications and other sources concerning the Klan. Contact Klanwatch at:

Klanwatch
P.O. Box 548
Montgomery, AL 36104
(202) 264-0286

National Association for the
Advancement of Colored People (NAACP)

The NAACP describes itself as an organization of persons of all races and religions who believe in the following: to achieve equal rights through the democratic process and eliminate racial prejudice by removing racial discrimination in housing, employment, voting, schools, the courts, transportation, recreation, prisons, and business enterprises. The association sponsors the NAACP National Housing Corporation to assist in the development of low- and moderate-income housing for families. The NAACP has about 1,800 local groups. For information on how you can volunteer for the association, look in your local telephone directory under National Association for the Advancement of Colored People, or contact their headquarters in Baltimore, Maryland:

National Association for the Advancement
of Colored People
4805 Mount Hope Drive
Baltimore, MD 21215
(410) 358-8900

National Council of La Raza (NCLR)

The National Council of La Raza works to improve opportunities for Hispanic Americans through addressing the problems of poverty and discrimination. Contact NCLR at:

National Council of La Raza
810 First St. NW, Suite 300
Washington, DC 20002
(202) 783-1670

National Urban League (NUL)

NUL is a nonpartisan community service agency that aims to eliminate racial segregation and discrimination. The league includes 113 local groups of civic, professional, business, labor, and religious leaders. It provides direct service in employment, housing, education, social welfare, health, family planning, mental retardation, law and consumer affairs, youth and student affairs, labor affairs, veterans affairs, and business development. For information on volunteering, look in your local telephone directory under National Urban League or contact their headquarters in New York City.

National Urban League
500 East 62nd St.
New York, NY 10021
(212) 310-9000

People for the American Way (PFAW)

PFAW is a nonpartisan organization of religious, business, media, and labor figures committed to reaffirming the traditional American values of pluralism, diversity, and freedom of expression and religion. PFAW believes that the individual matters and that Americans must strengthen the things that unite them. Contact PFAW's office in Washington, DC to find out how you can volunteer:

People for the American Way
2000 M St. NW, Suite 400
Washington, DC 20036
(202) 467-4999

Polish-American Guardian Society

This organization of Americans of Polish descent works to protect the name, reputation, and character of Polish-Americans. Contact them at:

Polish-American Guardian Society
8861 Wheeler Drive
Orland Park, IL 60462
(708) 403-9492

Puerto Rican Legal Defense and Education Fund (PRLDEF)

This fund works to protect and promote the civil rights of Puerto Ricans and other Latinos, and to increase the number of minority lawyers. To find out how you can help, call the fund's toll free number or contact them at:

Puerto Rican Legal Defense and Education Fund
99 Hudson St., 14th Floor
New York, NY 10013
(212) 219-3360
(800) 328-2322

Southern Christian Leadership Council (SCLC)

Founded in 1957, SCLC is a nonsectarian coordinating and service agency seeking the integration of African-Americans into all aspects of American life. SCLC is particularly active in the 16 southern and border states. Contact their office in Atlanta to find out how you can help:

Southern Christian Leadership Council
334 Auburn Ave. NE
Atlanta, GA 30303
(404) 522-1420

35

VOLUNTEER FOR HUMAN RIGHTS

Volunteers are an important part of the human rights movement, which works to make sure that the Universal Declaration of Human Rights is kept worldwide. Throughout the world, thousands of political prisoners have their rights violated every day, so the need for protection of human rights is ongoing. Here are just some of the organizations working to protect all human rights.

Amnesty International of the U.S.A. (AIUSA)

Amnesty International includes 400 local groups in the United States that work to release men and women detained anywhere for their conscientiously held beliefs, color, ethnic origin, sex, religion, or language, provided they have never used or advocated violence. The recipient of the 1977 Nobel Peace Prize, Amnesty International opposes torture, "disappearances," and executions and advocates fair and prompt trials for all political prisoners. AIUSA works cooperatively with other organizations such as the United Nations, the Council of Europe, and the Organization of African Unity. To find out how you can volunteer, contact AIUSA's office in New York.

Amnesty International of the U.S.A.
322 Eighth Ave.
New York, NY 10001
(212) 807-8400

Center of Concern (CC)

Center of Concern is a Catholic organization that works with grassroots and international networks to show the connections between global and local justice. Contact them at:

Center of Concern
3700 13th St. NE
Washington, DC 20017
(202) 635-2757

Committee of Concerned Scientists (CCS)

CCS is an organization of scholars united for the "protection and advancement of the scientific and human rights of scientists throughout the world." Contact CCS at:

Committee of Concerned Scientists
33-34 208th St.
Bayside, NY 11364
(718) 229-2813

Congressional Human Rights Caucus (CHRC)

This bipartisan caucus of the House of Representatives is concerned with human rights abuses around the world. The caucus coordinates the efforts of the members of Congress to end such abuses and to secure freedom from religious, ethnic, cultural, or political persecution.

Congressional Human Rights Caucus
U.S. Congress
H2-590, Ford House Office Building
Washington, DC 20515
(202) 226-4040

Human Rights Watch (HRW)

HRW promotes and monitors human rights worldwide. Among other things, it evaluates the human rights practices of governments in accordance with standards recognized by international laws and agreements including the United Nations Declaration of Human Rights and the Helsinki Accords. HRW also monitors the practices of nongovernmental groups such as guerilla organizations. HRW works in coordination with other agencies such as the Organization of American States and the United Nations.

Human Rights Watch
485 Fifth Ave., 3rd Floor
New York, NY 10017
(212) 972-8400

Lawyers Committee for Human Rights (LCHR)

This public interest law center and its volunteer lawyers work to promote international human rights and refugee law and legal procedures. LCHR is involved in the pro bono representation of indigent political asylum applicants in the United States. LCHR sponsors the Lawyer-to-Lawyer network, which includes volunteer lawyers in 90 countries. Contact LCHR at:

Lawyers Committee for Human Rights
330 Seventh Ave., 10th Floor
New York, NY 10001
(212) 629-6170

Physicians for Human Rights (PHR)

PHR's goal is to bring the skills of the medical profession to the protection of human rights. It has conducted over 50 missions to 35 countries. It works to prevent the participation of doctors in torture, to defend imprisoned health professionals, and to prevent physical and psychological abuse of citizens by governments. Contact PHR at:

Physicians for Human Rights
100 Boylston St., Suite 702
Boston, MA 02116
(617) 695-0041

36

VOLUNTEER FOR WOMEN'S RIGHTS AND WOMEN'S ISSUES

When you volunteer to work on women's issues you are volunteering to help over half of the population of the world gain equal status with the other half. The following organizations work on a range of issues important to women, including women's rights, the end to prostitution, career development, and the development of small income-generating businesses run by women in third world countries.

International Women's Rights Action Watch (IWRAW)
This network of activists and academics monitors changes in laws and policies according to the Convention on the Elimination of All Forms of Discrimination Against Women, which has been ratified by over 100 nations. The convention sets standards for achieving equality for women. Contact IWRAW at:

International Women's Rights Action Watch
University of Minnesota
Humphrey Institute of Public Affairs
301 19th Ave. South
Minneapolis, MN 55455
(612) 625-5093

National Action Forum for Midlife and Older Women (NAFMOW)
NAFMOW is a group concerned with upgrading the quality of life for women over 40 years of age. It works to

increase the public awareness of the status and needs of women in midlife and beyond. The forum publishes the newsletter *Hot Flash*. Contact NAFMOW at:

National Action Forum for Midlife and Older Women
Box 816
Stony Brook, NY 11790-0609

National Association for Women in Careers (NAFWIC)
This association provides support, networking, and skill development services for women to enhance their potential for greater success. NAFWIC includes eight regional groups, provides job referral, career planning, and conducts charitable programs. Contact them at:

National Association for Women in Careers
783 Forest Ridge Court
Oconomowoc, WI 53064
(414) 778-1919

National Organization for Women (NOW)
NOW works to bring women into full participation in the mainstream of society, in true equal partnership with men. NOW has programs in a number of areas such as economic rights, lesbian and gay rights, and ending violence against women. Contact NOW's office in Washington, DC to find a chapter near you:

NOW
1000 16th St. NW, Suite 700
Washington, DC 20036
(202) 331-0066

National Women's Mailing List (NWML)
The NWML is a project of the Women's Information Exchange. It works to utilize information technology to facilitate outreach, communication networking, and

179

resource sharing among women. Individual women and women's organizations can sign up to receive mail in a variety of interest areas such as politics, women's rights, health, sports, women's culture, and spirituality. Contact NWML at:

National Women's Mailing List
P.O. Box 68
Jenner, CA 95450
(707) 632-5763

Network for Professional Women (NPW)

NPW works to aid professional women in such areas as management of credit, employment networking, and reentering the workforce. Contact the network at:

Network for Professional Women
216 Main St.
Hartford, CT 06103
(203) 727-1988

The Nurturing Network (TNN)

This multinational organization of volunteers provides support for women facing unplanned pregnancies. The network makes referrals for legal assistance, adoption, and support services for over 6,000 mothers and their children. Call TNN's toll free number to find out how you can help:

The Nurturing Network
910 Main St., Suite 360
Boise, ID 83701
(218) 344-7200
(800) TNN-4MOM

Older Women's League (OWL)

This group of middle-aged and older women includes 120 local groups that address issues important to their well-being, such as health insurance, support for family caregivers, social security reform, effects of budget cuts on women, and self-sufficiency. OWL publishes the *OWL Observer*. To find a group near you, look in your local telephone directory under Older Women's League, or contact:

Older Women's League
666 11th St. NW, Suite 700
Washington, DC 20001
(202) 783-6686

PRIDE

This model program works to help women and teenage girls who have been involved in prostitution. PRIDE programs include information and referral, transitional housing, teenPRIDE groups for girls, court intervention, a 24-hour crisis line, and child care. PRIDE promotes changes in society that would stop the perpetuation of prostitution. Contact PRIDE's office in Minneapolis to find out how you can start a program in your area:

PRIDE
Family and Children's Services
3125 East Lake St.
Minneapolis, MN 55406
(612) 728-2062

Project Safe Run (PSR)

This model program trains dogs to protect women while walking or running by themselves. Dogs are kept at chapter houses where they can be checked out by women. Contact PSR at:

Project Safe Run
P.O. Box 22234
Eugene, OR 97402
(503) 345-8086

Women to the World (WW)
This multinational group assists poor women in developing countries with management training for small income-generating projects. Contact WW at:

Women to the World
1730 N. Lynn St., Suite 500
Arlington, VA 22209
(703) 528-3046

Wa-Tan-Ye Clubs
Wa-Tan-Ye is a Native American word that means foremost. Wa-Tan-Ye Clubs are organizations of business and professional women who work to increase participation in community service. Contact them at:

Wa-Tan-Ye Clubs
808 North Kentucky
Mason City, IA 50401
(515) 423-4196

37

VOLUNTEER TO HELP MILITARY PERSONNEL AND VETERANS

This key covers volunteer programs for veterans and active duty military personnel and their families.

Programs for Veterans
The Veterans Administration has hundreds of hospitals and nursing homes throughout the United States. To find a VA volunteer program near you, look in your local telephone directory under Veterans Administration. Other veterans programs that welcome volunteers are:

Blinded American Veterans Foundation (BAVF)
BAVF provides a number of services to blinded veterans including distributing telescoping canes, job hunting assistance, and providing computer training. Contact BAVF at:

Blinded American Veterans Foundation
P.O. Box 65900
Washington, DC 20035-5900
(202) 462-4430

Blinded Veterans Association (BVA)
BVA serves as an advocate for blinded veterans, provides financial assistance to their children, and lobbies for legislation. Contact BVA at:

Blinded Veterans Association
477 H St. NW
Washington, DC 20001-2694
(202) 371-8880

Department of Veterans Affairs (VA)
Voluntary Services

This program of the federal Veterans Administration has been in operation for almost 50 years. Volunteers work in VA medical centers, outpatient programs, and nursing homes. The VA provides training and other supportive services for volunteers. For information, call your local VA hospital, nursing home or other center, or contact:

Volunteer Services
Department of Veterans Affairs
50 Irving St.
Washington, DC 20422
(202) 745-8320

Disabled American Veterans (DAV)

DAV chapters provide a full range of services to veterans, including help with claims, transportation to medical visits, and training. Look in your local telephone directory under Disabled American Veterans, or contact:

Disabled American Veterans
807 Main Ave.
Washington, DC 20024
(202) 554-3501

Help Hospitalized Veterans (HHV)

HHV supplies arts and crafts materials to patients in military and veterans hospitals. Contact them at:

Help Hospitalized Veterans
2065 Kurtz St.
San Diego, CA 92110
(619) 291-5846

Operation Appreciation
Non-Commissioned Officers Association
of the United States (NCOA)

Operation Appreciation sends cards and other items of appreciation to hospitalized veterans during Christmas, Easter, and other holidays. To find out how you can take part in a program in your area, contact:

Operation Appreciation
225 N. Washington St.
Alexandria, VA 22314
(703) 549-0311

Paralyzed Veterans of America (PVA)

For 50 years PVA has been helping paralyzed veterans learn to live with their disabilities. For example, PVA sponsors wheelchair sports events such as basketball and track and field in chapters throughout the United States. To find a program near you, look in your telephone directory under Paralyzed Veterans of America, call PVA's toll free number or contact them at.

Paralyzed Veterans of America
801 18th St. NW
Washington, DC 20006
(800) 424-8200

The Veterans Bedside Network (VBN)

VBN volunteers work with hospitalized veterans in creative ways such as helping to produce radio and video programs in which the patients participate, and taking them to plays and other entertainment. Contact VBN at·

The Veterans Bedside Network
10 Fiske Place, Room 328
Mt. Vernon, NY 10550
(914) 699-6069

Programs for Active Military

To help active duty military personnel, contact a volunteer supervisor, family service center, or family service program at the military base closest to you. In addition, here are some other resources for volunteering with the armed forces:

Navy-Marine Corps Relief Society (NMCR)

The NMCR provides needed services to Navy and Marine Corps personnel. The society is a nonprofit organization that runs a number of programs including thrift shops, hospital visiting programs, and crisis intervention. To find out how you can help, contact:

Navy-Marine Corps Relief Society
801 North Randolph St., Room 1228
Arlington, VA 22203
(703) 696-4904

United Service Organization (USO)

The USO is well known for its excellent programs that help military personnel and their families cope with military life However, many people are not aware that the USO is not a federal program and it relies heavily on volunteers and funding from outside the government The USO has programs throughout the world providing services such as entertainment, community center activities, crisis intervention, counseling, day care centers, and canteens Contact the USO at

United Service Organization
Washington Navy Yard, Building 198
901 M St SE
Washington, DC 20374
(202) 610-5700

38

VOLUNTEER TO HELP CRIMINAL OFFENDERS REHABILITATE

There are many things you can do to help criminal offenders become more positive members of society. For example, you can teach a class or tutor individual prisoners; offer assistance in your area of expertise, such as counseling or legal work; help with drug or alcohol rehabilitation; or be an interested, nonjudgmental and friendly visitor.

To find a prison, dentention center, or parole program near you, check your local telephone directory under Department of Corrections or Department of Rehabilitation. Many states also have Offender Aid and Restoration (OAR) programs, which provide community-based alternatives to imprisonment. OAR programs welcome volunteers. Check in your local telephone directory to locate an Offender Aid and Restoration program in your area.

Prison Fellowship

Prison Fellowship is a Christian program that brings Bible classes into prisons, and helps out with other prisoner needs such as prerelease counseling. To find out about volunteering through Prison Fellowship, call their toll free number, or contact them at:

Prison Fellowship
P.O. Box 17500
Washington, DC 20041-0500
(703) 478-0100
(800) 497-0122

Prisoner Visitation and Support (PVS)

PVS provides volunteer opportunities in federal and military prisons exclusively. Volunteers usually visit a prison at least once a month. Contact PVS at:

Prisoner Visitation and Support
1501 Cherry St.
Philadelphia, PA 19102
(215) 241-7117

Volunteers in Prevention, Probation and Prisons Inc. (VIP)

VIP participants work one on one with individuals who are on probation. While the program is based in Detroit, VIP refers callers to similar programs around the country. Contact:

Volunteers in Prevention, Probation and Prisons Inc.
163 Madison Ave., Suite 120
Detroit, MI 48226
(313) 964-1110

39

VOLUNTEER AND TRAVEL IN THE UNITED STATES

The volunteer programs listed in this key all cover travel in the United States. Be sure to also check with the conservation, parks, or historical departments in the state where you are interested in volunteering and traveling. For example, the Illinois Department of Conservation in Springfield, Illinois runs several programs where volunteers work in parks assisting field biologists, serving as campground hosts, and running educational programs; the Indiana Division of State Parks runs volunteer programs where volunteers assist with landscaping and restoring trails; and the Kansas Archaeology Training Program runs projects where volunteers assist with archaeological excavation of prehistoric and historic sites.

Volunteer-and-travel programs that go outside the United States are covered in Key 40. Many international programs also have projects within the United States.

American Hiking Society (AHS)
AHS's goal is to preserve America's hiking trails. AHS volunteers spend two weeks helping with conservation projects in parks and national forests. All volunteers must be able to walk five to ten miles a day, and have experience with camping and backpacking. In order to find out how you can volunteer contact:

American Hiking Society
Volunteer Vacations
P.O. Box 20160
Washington, DC 20041
(301) 565-6704

Christian Appalachian Project (CAP)

CAP is an interdenominational Christian project that sponsors numerous relief programs to the people of Appalachia. Volunteers pay for their own transportation, and the project pays for housing and supplies food. To find out more about the program call CAP's toll free number or contact them at:

Christian Appalachian Project
235 Lexington St.
Lancaster, KY 40444
(606) 792-2132
(800) 755-5322

Colonial Williamsburg Foundation (CWF)

Colonial Williamsburg volunteers work in the restored area of Williamsburg, Virginia doing archaeological or laboratory work, or research. Volunteer projects range from introductory credit level courses at the College of William and Mary to unsupervised excavation projects for individuals with more experience. For more information contact:

Colonial Williamsburg Foundation
Department of Archaeological Research
P.O. Box 1776
Williamsburg, VA 23187
(804) 220-7330

Farm Hands-City Hands

Farm Hands volunteers perform a variety of tasks on farms in the Northeast. Projects include all aspects of farming, including making maple syrup or putting in crops. Contact Farm Hands at:

Farm Hands-City Hands
Green Chimneys
Putnam Lake Road
Brewster, NY 10509
(914) 279-2995, ext. 202

Lutheran Volunteer Corps (LVC)

LVC promotes living in a Christian community in the United States for a year of full-time service. Volunteers teach in inner city schools, work in homeless shelters, and perform other tasks to help low-income people. Participants may be of any faith. For more information contact:

Lutheran Volunteer Corps
1226 Vermont Ave. NW
Washington, DC 20005
(202) 387-3222

Mount Vernon Ladies Association

This project provides volunteer opportunities in archaeology and artifact processing in Mount Vernon, Virginia. Most volunteer projects take place in the summer. For more information contact:

Mount Vernon Ladies Association
Archaeology Department
Mount Vernon, VA 22121
(703) 780-2000, ext. 326

Oregon River Experiences Inc. (ORE)

ORE conducts educational white water trips in conjunction with Elderhostel (see page 198). Volunteers teach college level courses about the river and the surrounding area. Topics include biology, botany, river ecology, American Indian lore, and astronomy. For more information contact:

Oregon River Experiences
2 Jefferson Parkway #D7
Lake Oswego, OR 97035
(503) 697-8133

Passport in Time

This project provides archaeological or acting opportunities in national forests throughout the United States. Volunteers work directly with professional archaeologists or can appear as actors in living history presentations in national forests. To find out how you can volunteer, call Passport in Time's toll free number, or contact:

Passport in Time
P.O. Box 31315
Tucson, AZ 85751
(520) 722-2716
(800) 281-9176

Sierra Club Outing Department

The Sierra Club's volunteer travel programs involve trail maintenance, wilderness preservation, and archaeological work throughout the United States. Physicians receive waivers of costs and are not required to work when accompanying outings. (Although most physicians want to participate in every way they can.) To find out more about Sierra Club outings, contact:

Sierra Club Outing Department
730 Polk St.
San Francisco, CA 94109
(415) 776-2211

Sousson Foundation

The Sousson Foundation sponsors a number of restoration projects in national parks such as Yosemite and Kings Canyon. Volunteers may do everything from

192

planting trees to helping to build camp facilities. Contact the foundation at:

Sousson Foundation
3600 Ridge Road
Templeton, CA 93465
(805) 434-0299

Volunteers In Service To America (VISTA)
VISTA volunteers live and work among the poor in urban or rural areas of the United States. Participants may help the homeless, work on issues such as substance abuse prevention or literacy, or serve in other areas to help the poor. All volunteers receive training and a small amount of financial compensation. For information about the program, call VISTA's toll free number, or contact:

VISTA
Corporation for National and Community Service
1201 New York Ave. NW
Washington, DC 20525
(202) 606-5000
(800) 942-2677

Zoetic Research (ZR)
ZR sponsors whale research in the San Juan Islands, near Washington State. Contact the program at:

Zoetic Research
4770 Beaverton Valley Road
Friday Harbor, WA 98250
(360) 378-5767

40

VOLUNTEER AND TRAVEL OUTSIDE THE UNITED STATES

This key covers volunteering around the world, from Africa to Asia, from the Caribbean to the Arctic. Some words of caution: Most of these volunteer trips require commitment, courage, backbone, and emotional and physical strength. You should start out in relatively good health, because there is a good chance that you will be exposed to strenuous conditions that can test your stamina.

In short, many of these volunteer-and-travel programs, most of which involve travel to exotic ports of call, are not resort-like in any way. For example, you may be required to do heavy digging on an archaeological expedition, or teach in remote, impoverished, and disease-ridden areas of the world where you sleep at night in a grass hut.

None of these factors rule out volunteering on one of these projects because of age. In fact, one in ten Peace Corps volunteers is over age 55. (And the Peace Corps is known for its arduous tasks and situations.) It is important, however, to be aware of what you are getting into before you sign up for a month in Belize or the Sudan.

One valuable way of checking out these volunteer opportunities is to talk to at least two people who have taken the same trip that you are considering. You also might want to look into a range of programs before you sign up for a specific expedition or trip.

Here is a list of international programs that offer travel and volunteer work. For many, but not all, of these volunteer projects you will pay for your own transportation and other expenses.

Amigos de las Americas

This organization sponsors public health programs in Latin America. Volunteers must know some Spanish. Amigos provides training for projects such as inoculating people against yellow fever in remote areas and distributing needed medical supplies. To find out how you can help, call Amigos toll free number, or contact:

Amigos de las Americas
5618 Star Lane
Houston, TX 77057
(713) 782-5290
(800) 231-7796

B'nai B'rith

This international Jewish organization sponsors the Retirees in Israel program where volunteers study Hebrew and Jewish culture, and work in hospitals, nursing homes, schools, or other locations. To find out more about the program contact:

Retirees in Israel
1640 Rhode Island Ave. NW
Washington, DC 20036
(202) 857-6585

Caribbean Conservation Corporation (CCC)

CCC provides volunteer opportunities in Costa Rica and other areas conducting marine turtle research. The corporation's long range goal is to prevent the extinction of sea turtles. To find out how you can volunteer, contact:

Caribbean Conservation Corporation
P.O. Box 2866
Gainesville, FL 32606
(904) 373-6441

Christian Emergency Relief Team (CERT)

CERT volunteers spend about two weeks providing relief to those in need in remote locations within Africa, Asia, Central and Eastern Europe, and Latin America. Projects range from construction to providing medical care. To find out more about the program, call CERT's toll free number, or contact:

Christian Emergency Relief Team
P.O. Box 188058
Carlsbad, CA 92009
(619) 431-9890
(800) 541-4237

Christian Medical and Dental Society
Medical Group Missions

This organization welcomes volunteers with medical and dental backgrounds to work in clinics in poor areas throughout the world, including Africa, Asia, Latin America, and Eastern Europe. For more information about the program, contact:

Christian Medical and Dental Society
Medical Group Missions
P.O. Box 5
Bristol, TN 37621
(423) 844-1000

Citizen's Democracy Corps (CDC)
Business Entrepreneur Programs

This program places volunteers with business backgrounds in the former Soviet Union and other European countries to help companies with development. Participants work with companies for at least two months. To find out more about the program, call CDC's toll free number, or contact:

Citizen's Democracy Corps
Business Entrepreneur Programs
1735 I St. NW, Suite 720
Washington, DC 20006
(202) 872-0933
(800) 872-0933

Concern

This organization places volunteers with public health, medical, agriculture, engineering, and other professional backgrounds in Africa and Latin America. Participants work for about a year in community development in a variety of programs and receive a monthly stipend. To find out more about the program, call Concern's toll free number, or contact:

Concern
P.O. Box 1790
Santa Ana, CA 92702
(714) 953-8575
(800) CONCERN

Doctors Without Borders U.S.A. Inc.

Doctors Without Borders is the largest emergency medical aid organization in the world. Volunteers respond to disasters, wars, and other problems that cause medical crises anywhere in the world. They provide medical care to those in need, as well as training to the medical professionals in the country where they are assigned. Doctors Without Borders welcomes a wide range of doctors, nurses, and other medical professionals. Participants are given a small stipend. For more information, contact:

Doctors Without Borders U.S.A. Inc.
11 East 26th St., Suite 1904
New York, NY 10010
(212) 679-6800

Eco-Escuela de Espanol

Eco-Escuela volunteers work in community development in Guatemala while receiving language instruction. To learn more about the program, contact:

Eco-Escuela de Espanol
Conservation International
1015 18th St. NW, Suite 1000
Washington, DC 20036
(202) 973-2264

Elderhostel Service Programs

Elderhostel is a network of educational programs for adults age 60 and over. Elderhostel's Service Programs place participants in developing countries to teach, build housing, or perform other key tasks. To find out how you can volunteer, contact:

Elderhostel Service Programs
75 Federal St.
Boston, MA 02110
(617) 426-7788

Esperanca

Esperanca provides medical and dental care, including needed surgery, to the poor in developing countries. For more information about the program, contact:

Esperanca
1911 West Earll Drive
Phoenix, AZ 85015
(602) 252-7772

Fourth World Movement (FWM)
FWM volunteers work toward protecting human rights for poor Americans, as well as impoverished people living in Africa, Asia, Latin America, and other countries. Volunteers live in and help out in impoverished areas, which are also often remote. To find out more about the program, contact:

Fourth World Movement
7600 Willow Hill Drive
Landover, MD 20785
(301) 336-9489

Fellowship on Reconciliation Task Force on Latin America and the Caribbean
Volunteers work with victims of civil violence in Latin American and Caribbean countries. Participants must speak Spanish. For more information on the program, contact:

Fellowship on Reconciliation
Research Center
Task Force on Latin America and the Caribbean
515 Broadway
Santa Cruz, CA 95060
(408) 423-9089

Focus Inc.
This project is part of Loyola University's Department of Ophthalmology. Volunteers are certified ophthalmologists who perform surgery in Nigeria. To find out more about the program, contact:

Focus Inc.
Department of Ophthalmology
Loyola University Medical Center
Building 102
2160 S. First Ave.
Maywood, IL 60153
(708) 216-9598

Foundation for International Education

Through this project, volunteers work in English speaking countries, including Scotland and New Zealand. Participants usually teach or perform social work in conjunction with a teacher or counselor in the host country. To find out more about the program, contact:

Foundation for International Education
121 Cascade Court
River Falls, WI 54022
(715) 425-1774

Global Citizens Network

Global Citizens participants live with families in Guatemala, Kenya, and other countries, and work on community development projects. To find out more about the program, call Global Citizens' toll free number, or contact:

Global Citizens Network
1931 Iglehart Ave.
St. Paul, MN 55104
(612) 644-0969
(800) 644-9292

Global Service Corps

Global Service Corps volunteers donate their time on community development projects in Costa Rica, Guatemala, Kenya, and Thailand. Projects are conducted year-round and last from two weeks to a month. To find out more about the program, contact:

Global Service Corps
300 Broadway, Suite 28
San Francisco, CA 94133-3312
(415) 788-3666, ext. 128

Global Volunteers

This project's goals are to establish peace through international understanding. Volunteers work in the United States, Latin America, the South Pacific, and in other areas of the world. Tasks vary from tutoring to construction work on housing and clinics. To find out how you can help, call Global Volunteers' toll free number, or contact:

Global Volunteers
375 Little Canada Road
St. Paul, MN 55117
(612) 482-1074
(800) 487-1074

Health Volunteers Overseas (HVO)

HVO provides training to medical professionals in developing countries such as Africa, Asia, and Central and South America. To find out more information, contact:

Health Volunteers Overseas
Washington Station
P.O. Box 65157
Washington, DC 20035-5157
(202) 296-0928

International Eye Foundation (IEF)

IEF has projects throughout the third world that work to prevent blindness and to train local health workers in eye care. Volunteers must have a background in ophthalmology. To find out more about the program, contact:

International Eye Foundation
7801 Norfolk Ave.
Bethesda, MD 20814
(301) 986-1830

International Families
Volunteers for International Families help children living in Russian orphanages. Participants must have at least two years of college level Russian. They usually spend about a month working directly with children. To find out more about the program, contact:

International Families
214 Atlantic Highway
Northport, ME 04849
(207) 338-5165

International Medical Corps (IMC)
IMC volunteers provide medical care in devastated areas of the world, including Bosnia, Angola, and Cambodia. Participants are medical professionals or nonmedical individuals with international project experience. For more information, contact:

International Medical Corps
12233 West Olympic Blvd., Suite 280
Los Angeles, CA 90064-1052
(310) 826-7800

Jesuit Volunteers International (JVI)
JVI is a lay volunteer program that works to help people in developing countries such as Belize, Peru, and Nepal through teaching and other tasks. People of all faiths may volunteer with the group. To find out more about the program, contact:

Jesuit Volunteers International
P.O. Box 25478
Washington, DC 20007
(202) 687-1132

Jewish National Fund
Canadian American-Active Retirees in Israel (CA-ARI)

CA-ARI volunteers work in various capacities in Israel learning about the country and at the same time contributing to its future. Volunteers often perform forestry and community work. To find out more about the program, call CA-ARI's toll free number, or contact:

Jewish National Fund
Canadian American-Active Retirees in Israel
42 East 69th St.
New York, NY 10021-5093
(212) 879-9300
(800) 223-7798

Interplast

Interplast volunteers perform surgery on children and adults in developing countries who have birth deformities or crippling injuries. Interplast welcomes nonmedical volunteers to help with administrative tasks, as well as medical professionals. To find out more about the program, contact:

Interplast
300 B Pioneer Way
Mountain View, CA 94041
(415) 962-0123

Lost World Trading Company

The Lost World Trading Company runs year-round volunteer expeditions in archaeology and anthropology in Mexico, the Caribbean, and West Africa. Contact them at:

Lost World Trading Company
P.O. Box 365
Oakdale, CA 95361
(209) 847-5393

Mercy Corps International (MCI)

MCI volunteers provide emergency relief and community development in a number of countries including Honduras, Israel, Lebanon, and the Sudan. MCI will help participants raise funds to cover the costs of their trips. To find out how you can volunteer, call MCI's toll free number, or contact:

Mercy Corps International
3030 SW First Ave.
Portland, OR 97201
(503) 242-1032
(800) 292-3355

Midwest Medical Mission Inc.

This mission, based in Ohio, sends physicians and other medical professionals to the Dominican Republic to provide medical care to the needy. Nonmedical volunteers are also welcome to help with administrative tasks. Contact the mission at (419) 389-1239.

Oceanic Society Expeditions

Volunteers for the Oceanic Society help conduct research on dolphins, sea turtles, howler monkeys, and whales in California, Belize, Hawaii, Honduras, and Peru. Some trips involve scuba diving. To find out how you can help, call the society's toll free number, or contact:

Oceanic Society Expeditions
Fort Mason Center
Building E, Suite 230
San Francisco, CA 94123
(415) 441-1106
(800) 326-7491

Operation Smile International (OSI)

Operation Smile sends medical professionals around the world to perform reconstructive surgery on indigent children with deformities such as cleft palates. Contact OSI at:

Operation Smile International
717 Boush St.
Norfolk, VA 23510
(804) 625-0375

Partners of the Americas

This large and innovative volunteer program provides opportunities in international development and technical training. Partnerships are made between specific states or regions in the United States and a specific area in Latin America or the Caribbean. Volunteers then work with their counterparts in the partnership. Project tasks range from disaster relief to AIDS prevention. To find out what area your state is partners with and what opportunities are available, call the Partners toll free number, or contact:

Partners of the Americas
1424 K St. NW, Suite 700
Washington, DC 20005
(202) 628-3300
(800) 322-7844

Pax World Service

The Pax World Service runs tours that reflect the organization's goals of peace and reconciliation and the development of people. Volunteers may travel to Antiqua, Costa Rica, the Dominican Republic, and Honduras where projects range from planting trees to helping to install water purification systems.

Pax World Service
1111 16th St. NW, Suite 120
Washington, DC 20036
(202) 293-7290

Peace Corps

Peace Corps volunteers serve in more than 90 countries throughout the world for two years or more. They work on a mission of world peace, friendship, and sharing, and perform such tasks as agricultural development, education, engineering, forestry, health and medical care, industrial arts, and business development. Volunteers receive at least three months of training. One in ten Peace Corps volunteers is over age 55. To find out how you can volunteer, call the Peace Corps toll free number, or contact:

Peace Corps
1990 K St. NW
Washington, DC 20526
(800) 424-8580

Peacework

Peacework sponsors short-term international volunteer projects in developing countries around the world. Participants come from different countries and learn about global hunger and poverty, while performing a variety of community development tasks. For more information about Peacework, contact:

Peacework
305 Washington St. SW
Blacksburg, VA 24060
(540) 953-1376

Physicians for Peace Foundation

Physicians for Peace sends medical professionals around the world in the spirit of promoting international friendships and peace. For more information about the foundation, contact:

Physicians for Peace Foundation
229 West Bute St., Suite 820
Norfolk, VA 23510
(804) 625-7569

Presbyterian Church Mission Volunteers

Volunteers in this program travel in the United States and around the world to help people who are poor and in need of community development services. Participants need not be Presbyterian. To find out how you can volunteer, call the mission's toll free number, or contact:

Presbyterian Church Mission Volunteers
100 Witherspoon St.
Louisville, KY 40202
(502) 569-5295
(800) 779-6779

Project Concern International (PCI) Options Service

PCI's Options Service sends medical professionals to areas of need in the world. PCI publishes a bimonthly newsletter that lists volunteer opportunities. To receive the newsletter, or for more information, contact:

Project Concern International
Options Service
35550 Afton Road
San Diego, CA 92123
(619) 279-9690

Project HOPE

Project HOPE sends health professionals to train their counterparts around the world. (The HOPE in the organization's title comes from Health Opportunities for People Everywhere.) Projects range from providing the most basic medical care in remote communities to helping to develop sophisticated medical centers. For more information about Project Hope, call the project's toll free number, or contact:

Project HOPE
Carter Hall
Health Sciences Education Center
Millwood, VA 22646
(703) 837-2100
(800) 544-4673

Sea Turtle Restoration Project
Earth Island Institute

Participants in the Sea Turtle Restoration Project work with environmentalists observing the behavior of Ridley sea turtles on the beaches of Costa Rica, Mexico, and Nicaragua. To find out how you can volunteer, call the project's toll free number, or contact:

Sea Turtle Restoration Project
Earth Island Institute
300 Broadway, Suite 28
San Francisco, CA 94133
(415) 788-3666
(800) 859-SAVE

Smithsonian Research Expeditions
The Smithsonian Associates

The Smithsonian Associates sponsors these expeditions, which give volunteers opportunities to work with researchers in a variety of areas. Expeditions may be in the United States, Australia, Bali, Costa Rica, or other countries and cover such topics as anthropology, archaeology, astronomy, biology, environmental issues, photographic documentation, social science, and marine and wildlife ecology. For information about the expeditions, contact:

Smithsonian Research Expeditions
The Smithsonian Associates
490 L'Enfant Plaza SW, Suite 4210
Washington, DC 20560
(202) 287-3210

University of California Research Expeditions Program (UREP)

UREP is an international organization that sponsors projects around the world, as well as in the United States. Project goals are to preserve the world's natural and cultural resources. Volunteers may work in the areas of archaeology, paleontology, and social science, but do not need any special training. For more information, contact:

University of California Research Expeditions
 Program
University of California at Berkeley
2223 Fulton St.
Berkeley, CA 94720
(510) 642-6586

Volunteers for Israel

Volunteers for Israel help with the national effort of the Jewish people in Israel. Volunteer projects depend on the present needs of the people of Israel and they run for 23 days. People of all faiths and political backgrounds are welcome to volunteer. For more information about the program, contact:

Volunteers for Israel
330 West 42nd St., Suite 1818
New York, NY 10036
(212) 643-4848

Volunteers in Overseas Cooperative Assistance (VOCA)

VOCA works to increase the economics of small and medium-sized agriculture-based businesses around the world. Volunteers provide technical assistance to agribusinesses in Africa, Asia, the Near East, Latin America, and other countries. For information about the program, call VOCA's toll free number, or contact:

Volunteers in Overseas Cooperative Assistance
50 F St. NW, Suite 1075
Washington, DC 20001
(202) 383-4961
(800) 929-VOCA

Volunteers for Peace (VFP)

Volunteers for Peace sponsors workcamps in countries around the world, as well as the United States. Participants work on a variety of community development projects. For more information about the program, contact:

Volunteers for Peace
International Workcamps
43 Tiffany Road
Belmont, VT 05730
(802) 259-2759

WorldTeach

WorldTeach volunteers teach English to Chinese students in Shanghai and in the process they learn Chinese. No teaching experience is necessary to apply. While many volunteers are college students, older people are wel-

come. For more information about the program, call
WorldTeach's toll free number, or contact:

WorldTeach
Harvard Institute for International Development
1 Eliot St.
Cambridge, MA 02138
(617) 495-5527
(800) 4TEACH0

41

NATIONAL RESOURCES FOR VOLUNTEERING

Virtually all states and large cities have large and well-organized volunteer centers, which are invaluable resources for locating opportunities in your area. You will find such centers listed in your local telephone directory under United Way, Volunteer Center, Volunteer Action, or Volunteer Bureau.

In addition, the national resources listed below can guide you to volunteer programs in your local area or assist you in starting new programs.

American Red Cross

The American Red Cross is known as the premier volunteer emergency services organization. In operation over 130 years, it has 2,600 chapters in the United States. Volunteers perform a wide variety of services including assisting in blood centers, teaching first aid, and helping to repair homes that were damaged by natural causes. They also help people contact loved ones in any part of the world if disaster strikes. Training is provided for volunteers.

American Red Cross
National Headquarters
Seventh and D Sts. NW
Washington, DC 20006
(202) 737-8300

Catholic Charities

This network of agencies provides services to those in need. It includes over 1,400 local agencies. Participants do not need to be Catholic. Types of programs volunteers can work in are: adoption, counseling, employment programs, housing, food banks and other homeless programs, pregnancy services, and refugee and immigration services. To find a program near you, look in your local telephone directory under Catholic Charities, or contact:

Catholic Charities
3838 Cathedral Lane
Arlington, VA 22203
(703) 841-2531

City Cares

This organization arranges volunteer activities for people with busy lives. Volunteers may perform a variety of activities early in the morning before work, on week nights, or weekends. These are just some of the many activities volunteers can perform through City Cares: serving meals in shelters, reading to people who are blind, delivering meals, or cleaning up parks. Such programs may be listed in your phone book under (Your City) Cares or Hands on (Your City). Contact:

City Cares of America
1737 H St. NW
Washington, DC 20006
(202) 887-0500

Family Service America

This agency works to improve family life. Family Service America includes 280 local agencies, which reflect the needs of their local communities. Examples of services are crisis hotlines, day care centers, and family counseling.

Call their toll free number to find a program near you, or contact:

Family Service America
11700 W. Lake Park Drive
Milwaukee, WI 53224
(414) 359-1040
(800) 221-2681

Four-One-One

Four-One-One is a national clearinghouse on volunteerism. The organization provides resources for planning, designing, and managing successful volunteer programs. Contact the clearinghouse at:

Four-One-One
7304 Beverly St.
Annandale, VA 22003
(703) 354-6270

Jewish Community Centers

Volunteers of all faiths work through these programs to meet local needs. They may provide food for the homeless, visit hospital and nursing home patients, help resettle Jewish families from other countries, or provide other important community services. To locate a program near you, look in your local telephone directory under Jewish Community Center. Your local synagogue will also know of community centers in your area.

Jewish Community Centers Association
 of North America
15 East 26th St., 10th Floor
New York, NY 10010-1579
(212) 532-4949

Jewish Family and Children's Agencies
These agencies provide services such as counseling to children and families. Call their toll free number to find a program near you, or contact:

Association of Jewish Family and Children's Agencies
P.O. Box 248
Kendall Park, NJ 08824-0248
(908) 821-0909
(800) 634-7346

Independent Sector (IS)
The IS is a coalition of about 800 corporations, foundations, and voluntary organizations. Their mission is to create a forum for the promotion of volunteerism. They disseminate research material on volunteering. The Independent Sector is a good resource for learning about funding-related issues for volunteer programs.

Independent Sector
1828 L St. NW
Washington, DC 20036
(202) 223-8100

National Urban League
Through more than a hundred affiliates in the United States, the National Urban League works to secure equal opportunities for African-Americans and other minorities. The National Urban League welcomes volunteers. Look in your local phone book to see if there is an affiliate in your area, or contact:

National Urban League
The Equal Opportunity Building
500 East 62nd St.
New York, NY 10021
(212) 310-9000

Points of Light Foundation

This foundation assists volunteer programs in expanding and improving. Points of Light has a network of about 400 affiliated volunteer centers. Call their toll free number to find a program near you.

Points of Light Foundation
1737 H St. NW
Washington, DC 20006
(202) 223-9186
(800) 879-5400

Salvation Army

This organization focuses on a love of God and helping people in need. It includes over 10,000 centers in the United States, which provide emergency shelter for the homeless, emergency shelter for victims of crime, counseling, crisis hotlines, disaster services, and other programs to help people. For a Salvation Army program near you look in your local phone book, or contact:

The Salvation Army
National Headquarters
615 Slaters Lane
P.O. Box 269
Alexandria, VA 22313
(703) 684-5500

United Way

Your local United Way agency has a list of programs it sponsors in your area. There are over 2,100 United Way organizations in communities throughout the United States, and almost 50,000 agencies receive United Way support. Check in your local phone book under United Way for the listing of an office near you, or contact:

United Way
701 North Fairfax St.
Alexandria, VA 22314-2045
(703) 836-7100

Volunteers of America (VOA)

This Christian-based organization welcomes volunteers of any religious orientation. VOA offers a variety of programs in over 300 communities in the United States. Examples of the types of programs they offer are: meals to homebound people, necessary items for the needy, AIDS support programs, counseling, suicide prevention, job training, emergency shelters, and housing programs. To find a program near you, look for Volunteers of America in your local phone book or call their toll free number:

Volunteers of America
3939 North Causeway Blvd., Suite 400
Metairie, LA 70002
(504) 837-2652
(800) 899-0089

The Young Men's Christian Association of the United States of America (YMCA)

There are over 2,000 YMCAs across the country providing community programs for men and women of all ages. Each YMCA is run by a volunteer board. Check with the YMCA near you to see what programs it offers, call their toll free number, or contact:

YMCA of the U.S.A.
101 North Wacker Drive
Chicago, IL 60606
(312) 977-0031
(800) 872-9622

The Young Women's Christian Association
of the United States of America (YWCA)

The YWCA has over 4,000 facilities nationwide. Programs focus on empowering women of all ages. Check with the YWCA near you to see what programs it offers, or contact:

YWCA of the U.S.A.
726 Broadway
New York, NY 10003
(212) 614-2700

INDEX

224